THE JOURNEY

GEMMA ELIZABETH WILLIAMS & CO

Published in 2025 by The Easiest Choice Publishing

Copyright ©Gemma Elizabeth Williams

The following chapters are Gemma Elizabeth Williams & Co's intellectual property and written in the author's own words.

All rights reserved.
The printed book is distributed worldwide. No part of this book may be used, replicated or reproduced, stored in a retrieval system, or transmitted in any form or by any means, electronic, mechanical, photocopying, recording, or otherwise, without the written permission of the author(s). Quotations of no more than 25 words are permitted, but only if used solely for the purposes of critical articles or reviews.

ISBN: 978-1-0683862-1-3

Although the author and publisher have made every effort to ensure that the information in this book is correct at the time of going to print, the author and publisher do not assume and therefore disclaim liability to any party. The author and the publisher will not be held responsible for any loss or damage save for that caused by their negligence.

Although the author and the publisher have made every reasonable attempt to achieve accuracy in the content of this book, they assume no responsibility for errors or omissions.

Page design and typesetting by

The Easiest Choice Publishing

Contents

Foreword: *By Gemma Elizabeth Williams* — 5
Chapter One: *By Gemma Elizabeth Williams* — 7
Chapter Two: *By Rachel Harper* — 20
Chapter Three: *By Sian Taylor* — 29
Chapter Four: *By Helen Stephens* — 38
Chapter Five: *By Sadie Hallett-Chambers* — 47
Chapter Six: *By Alicia Harris* — 57
Chapter Seven: *By Lynsey Cowie* — 66
Chapter Eight: *By Sabrina Faulkner* — 76
Chapter Nine: *By Sharon Bedford* — 85
Chapter Ten: *By Harriet Clay* — 96
Chapter Eleven: *By Kelley Crocker* — 106
Chapter Twelve: *By Nat Simpkin* — 115
Chapter Thirteen: *By Deanne Millis* — 124
Chapter Fourteen: *By Tara Haley* — 134
Chapter Fifteen: *By Karen Preston* — 144
Chapter Sixteen: *By Lynden Riley* — 153
Chapter Seventeen: *By Charlene Cransten* — 162
Chapter Eighteen: *By Pixie Inanna* — 169
Chapter Nineteen: *By Shelley Fifer Richardson* — 178
Chapter Twenty: *By Lorna Hammond* — 187
Chapter Twenty-one: *By Leigh Stierle* — 197
Chapter Twenty-two: *By Donna Talbot* — 204
Chapter Twenty-three: *By Shirley Bailey* — 212

Trigger Warning: Some of the chapters in this book discuss sensitive subjects including sexual abuse, childhood abuse, drug abuse and addiction, suicide, rape, sex work, and knife crime. Please be mindful of this before reading.

Disclaimer: All authors in this book are not doctors or providing medical recommendations. This book shares personal experiences and is intended for informational purposes only. It is not a substitute for medical advice, diagnosis or treatment. Never ignore professional medical advice in seeking treatment.

These stories are written by real women in their own words.

Foreword

By Gemma Elizabeth Williams

Welcome to 'The Journey' an incredible book of self-discovery and empowerment! Writing a book has been a dream of mine for many years and also of the ladies who took part in this collaboration. I always wanted to create a book of real-life stories, so decided to collaborate with other inspiring women to make that happen.

In this book collaboration I want to inspire and uplift women from all walks of life. No matter the challenges you may be facing, always remember that the light at the end of the tunnel is YOU. You possess the strength and resilience to overcome any obstacle, and this book is a testament to that.

No matter what you've been through or are going through you have the strength and power within you to change your reality. Within these pages, you will find a collection of diverse chapters penned by remarkable women who have transformed their pain into power. Each story is unique, yet they all share a common thread, the unwavering determination to rise above adversity and create a brighter future.

While we are all still navigating our individual paths, each day presents an opportunity for growth and self-improvement as we strive to become the best versions of ourselves. My vision for this collaboration was to unite incredible women, each with their own distinct experiences, and to share their powerful narratives with the world.

These stories serve as a beacon of hope and inspiration for others, reminding us that it is never too late to start again and rewrite our own stories. I wanted to give others hope and inspiration that it's never too late to turn your life around.

I truly hope that as you delve into this book, you find as much joy and inspiration in reading it as we did in creating it. Together, let's celebrate our journeys, empower one another, continue to shine bright, and support each other on the journey of life. Enjoy!

Chapter One

By Gemma Elizabeth Williams

I'm Gemma Elizabeth Williams, a proud mother of two boys and a grandmother to two lovely granddaughters. I live in a small town called Bedford. I am a dedicated manifesting, mindset and spiritual mentor, as well as a psychic, reiki master and energy healing course creator. My passion for empowering women drives my work and I am honoured to have guided thousands of women on their journey of transformation. Together we've harnessed the power of inner healing and reprogramming limiting beliefs, allowing women to step confidently into their power and manifest the lives they truly desire and deserve.

Broken

In 2009, my world shattered. I lost my nan, the absolute rock of my life, and just a year later, my grandad followed, leading to a completely broken heart. My nan was more than just a grandmother, she was my best friend, my confidante. I couldn't imagine a life without them both, and now they were both gone. The pain inside me was unlike anything I had ever experienced. It was a deep ache that settled in my heart, marking the beginning of my journey into my rock bottom. Yet, unknown in the darkness it also sparked the first flickers of my awakening.

I had already faced the loss of my dad to suicide when I was just 21. Although his absence had left scars, he hadn't been a constant presence in my life, and I had learned to grieve him over the years, even while he was still alive. But losing my nan and grandad was an entirely different pain. They were two of the most vital figures in my existence, and suddenly they were gone.

The Journey

I was used to seeing my nan weekly and always had done since I was a child, and we spoke on the phone multiple times a day. The void they left was profound, a silence that echoed in every corner of my heart. Their absence was not just a loss, it was the end of an era, a moment that would redefine my journey forever.

At that time, I had two young boys at home, and I wasn't working. While they were at school, I found myself in a world of silence, with no more of the lively conversations I used to have with my nan. Instead of picking up the phone or meeting her in town, I was left alone. I spiralled deeper into depression, and I just couldn't pull myself out of it, to be honest I didn't even know how.

There were days when I didn't even have the energy to get dressed, each morning feeling heavier than the last. The weight of my grief wrapped around me like a thick fog, suffocating and inescapable. I was in a relationship that was slowly crumbling under the strain of my emotional turmoil. My mind was a chaotic mess, lost in the depths of sorrow, and eventually, it all became too much to bear. In the end, I made the difficult decision to separate from my partner and my best friend. The connection we once shared faded as my grief consumed me, leaving me feeling isolated and adrift. The journey through this darkness was not just about losing my nan and grandad, it was also about confronting the fractures in my own life and the painful realisations that followed.

Lost

I started going out on weekends when my boys were with their dad. It was as if I had suddenly realised that life was too short, and all I wanted was to have some fun. But deep down, I was just trying to escape the pain of losing my nan and grandad. Their absence weighed heavily on my heart, and the weekends became a temporary distraction from the grief.

The Journey

A few months later, I met a guy who approached me with charm and confidence, chatting me up effortlessly. He asked for my number, and despite a warning voice whispering in my mind that this man would turn my world upside down, I ignored it and handed over my number. He made me laugh, and in a time when I felt so low, I was desperate for any kind of happiness.

It didn't take long for the cracks to show in this new relationship. Toxic traits emerged, and I soon found myself the target of his violence. I remember the first time when I was preparing to leave him, he dropped to his knees, begging me to stay. Something about him reminded me of my dad, and I thought perhaps I could help him change, that I could help him heal. At that stage of my journey, I was completely unaware of how much I also needed healing within myself.

I stayed in this toxic relationship for three long years. It was a rollercoaster filled with ups and downs, tears and laughter, and an ever-present shadow of abuse. The heartbreaking truth was that, because of my father's treatment of my mother, I had come to view this turmoil as normal.

Even though that voice within me repeatedly told me I deserved better, the lack of self-love, self-worth, and self-esteem kept me in this situation. I was told over and over that I would be nothing without him, that no one would ever want or love me. Slowly but surely, I began to believe his lies.

The absence of self-love within me created a deep craving for affection, blinding me to the reality that I was losing myself more with each passing day. I clung desperately to the hope that I could change him, that I could fix the pain he inflicted when he turned on me. The fleeting moments of joy, when he attempted to make up for his toxic behaviour were intoxicating, and the fear of being alone and the unknown scared me; fear was controlling me from all angles.

As I navigated this darkness, I was trapped in a cycle and desperately yearning for something better while feeling unworthy of it. It was a rock bottom I couldn't yet see, I was completely lost, but with every tear and every moment of laughter that masked the pain, I was unknowingly on the verge of a journey towards healing and self-discovery.

I vividly recall those moments after heated arguments, when I found myself with a pillow pressed over my face, struggling to breathe. His voice would echo in my ears, threatening, "I'm going to kill you." As he would lift the pillow I would gasp for breath and before I knew it the pillow was back over my face.

In my desperation, I would pray to God for help, pleading for the universe to fill my heart with hatred and grant me the strength to walk away from him, I was filled with fear, scared and felt like I had no one to turn to. Although I did, but part of me felt embarrassed as the old Gemma would have never of put up with kind of behaviour. I didn't know how to tell anyone what I was going through.

His abuse was insidious and cunning, he knew how to inflict pain without leaving visible marks, except for the bruises on my arms where he would grip me tightly. He would drag me through his house by my hair, hurling insults, suffocating me with pillows, and once, he even threw me into his backyard, completely exposed. Yet, no matter how much he hurt me, I found myself apologising, believing his claims that I was the cause of his rage. Also scared if I didn't apologise what he might do next. I felt like a shadow of my former self. Once, I had thought of myself as strong, but now I felt utterly weak, lost, and unsure of who I was. The Gemma I once knew wasn't there anymore.

Rock Bottom

I found myself trapped in a cycle with someone who had caused me so much pain until I discovered Reiki. I learned Level One to aid my inner healing. After my attunement I experienced a beautiful sense of inner peace, however the toxicity of our relationship soon overshadowed that tranquillity. I could feel a powerful energy urging me to break away from him, yet the fear of being alone and unlovable kept me clinging to what had become a damaging trauma bond.

As I progressed to Level Two, I began to gain strength and clarity. I realised that he and I were on completely different wavelengths, and our relationship was destined to fail. This sparked a journey of acceptance within me, which was challenging due to my low self-esteem and fear of the unknown. I could sense my ancestors and spirit guides were supporting me.

Having been psychic since childhood, I had never truly harnessed my abilities until now. My intuition persistently warned me that he was seeing someone else behind my back, I felt it strongly, even without proof. Ironically, he often accused me of cheating on him, despite knowing my whereabouts at all times. I recall telling him, "You're accusing me because it's what you're doing," which would only provoke his rage and lead to violent outbursts.

I began to understand that some things were better left unsaid, as they would only trigger his anger, which he would then take out on me. Meditation and Reiki became my lifelines. One afternoon while meditating, I was visited by one of my spirit guides, who was holding a mobile phone. I asked what it was for, and they instructed me to text him from a different number.

Coming out of the meditation, I felt a mix of excitement, fear, and anxiety. I went to the shop, purchased a SIM card, and sent him a message stating that I was going to tell Gemma everything. His response was chilling. "You do that, and I will come to Northampton and kill you." In that moment, I finally had proof of the situation I was in. This revelation gave me a valid reason to leave, as until then, I had been making excuses to stay. It marked the beginning of my rock bottom. In that instant, I realised just how lost and unhealed I truly was. I hadn't processed the loss of my grandparents or the breakup with my children's father. What had I done to my life? I had thrown everything I once knew anyway.

It was a complete disaster. I felt like a broken woman, and I didn't want to continue living in this state anymore. I didn't want to feel this pain anymore. I had lost myself and felt like my world had fallen apart, I had hit my version of rock bottom.

My Awakening

Walking away was a challenge, as I was still bound by a trauma connection to him, believing that I loved him. In the first three weeks, I struggled to eat and cried myself to sleep, wondering how my life had spiralled into such chaos. I felt terrified about my future and even began to think my children would be better off without me, I felt like a complete let down and failure also as a mother. I just didn't feel good enough in any area of my life.

Despite our separation, the abuse persisted, with him continually threatening me. He repeatedly said he would throw acid in my face so that no man would ever look at me again. He accused me of being unfaithful with his friend, screaming at me over the phone and hurling insults. The emotional and mental abuse was relentless, leaving me riddled with anxiety, causing me to lose weight and drop to a size 6. This went on for several months.

Eventually, I found the courage to call the police. Due to his violent history, he was taken to court and ordered not to contact me again. I vividly recall sitting at my dining room table, crying and wishing for a different life, shouting that things needed to change. Suddenly, I heard a male voice firmly say, "No, Gem, you need to change." That was the moment my awakening began. I wiped my tears and had a powerful realisation, I didn't love or respect myself, nor did I feel worthy—I never had.

Having dyslexia, I faced bullying in school, and my parents' separation meant I saw little of my father afterward. I realised I needed inner child healing. I sought love from men because my dad wasn't there; my first boyfriend moved away, highlighting my deep-seated abandonment issues. I was often insecure and jealous.

I expressed to my spirit guides that I just wanted someone to love me, and the response I received was, "How can someone love you when you don't love yourself?" That was my lightbulb moment. I understood that I needed to focus on inner healing and self-work. Finding love from someone else wasn't the solution—loving myself was.

Healing meant recognising my worth and respecting myself, letting go of the past, and embracing forgiveness as the key to my freedom. The awakening had begun. I knew the journey wouldn't be easy and that there would be no quick fixes, but I was eager to embark on it, feeling reassured that I would be okay. The universe had my back.

I endured a great deal of pain and trauma throughout my life, leading me to believe that it was all over. However, it turned out to be just the beginning of my journey to rebuild my life in the way I truly desired. Nothing was going to stop me, and I started to turn my pain into power.

Transformation And Manifestation

I understood that turning my pain into power would be a transformative journey, and I poured my heart and soul into inner healing, manifestation, and personal growth. I began to shift my mindset and reprogram my limiting beliefs. Initially, I focused on manifesting small things, which eventually grew into larger and more fulfilling experiences. With guidance from my spirit guides, I was changing my life.

Despite many people around me thinking I had completely lost my way by talking about spirit guides and the Universe, I felt a deep inner certainty. I even had an incredible dream where one of my spirit guides assured me that I was on the right path. It was in that moment that I made a commitment to the Universe to dedicate my life to teaching the true secrets of manifestation, even though I wasn't sure how I would accomplish this.

I envisioned having my own crystal shop and offering energy healing to others, so I put that intention out into the Universe. As a child, I had dreamed of owning my grandfather's greengrocers, a place where I had worked as a teenager. I felt my grandfather was supporting me on this journey, as he frequently appeared in my dreams.

I was a single mother; I was over £20,000 in debt and surviving on just £120 a week. However, I sensed that change was imminent. I ultimately manifested the ideal shop that had once belonged to my grandfather on my father's side back in the 1970s, even though I had never met him. While I didn't manifest my grandfather's shop directly, I received unexpected financial gifts, making the opening of my shop a dream come true in 2015. This marked the beginning of my mission to help others heal and teach the true secrets of manifestation.

I started offering weekly spiritual development mentoring sessions, angel card readings, Reiki energy healing, sound healings, and teaching Reiki. I eventually ventured into hosting spiritual retreats. Through inner healing and the application of various tools, I completely transformed my life. I began connecting with new people on Facebook, and many expressed a desire to live closer so they could participate in everything I offered at my shop. This inspired me to create my online VIP Manifesting Academy, allowing women to engage from the comfort of their own homes.

I could easily write an entire book about everything I've manifested since embarking on this journey, as well as the incredible transformations the women in my academy have experienced. I have helped thousands of women around the world completely change their lives and now live a life of fulfilment, through manifesting the life they desire.

My Dream Life

Reflecting on my journey and everything I've experienced; I am filled with gratitude. The path has often been incredibly challenging and painful since childhood, but the transformation has been utterly life changing.

I've faced many painful situations, with the adoption of my granddaughter being the most heart-wrenching for both me and my son. Had I not already shifted my mindset, I honestly don't know how I would have coped or supported my son through such a heartbreaking time. One important lesson I've learned on this earthly journey is that we all encounter various painful experiences—some due to our own choices and others beyond our control. However, what we can control is how we respond.

It opened my eyes to the corruption within the system and social services. While not all social workers are at fault, some certainly are. My son wasn't given the opportunity to be a father, and they used his ADHD and school behaviour against him. They also targeted me, referencing my father's suicide to claim that our family had mental health issues, and mentioned that I had called the police on my ex-partner, who had nothing to do with my children. My family and I went to court to fight for the custody of my granddaughter. My parents were deemed too old, and my cousin was told she had too many children for my granddaughter Scarlett to be a priority. Ironically, the family that adopted her also had children of their own. The barrister shockingly stated that my granddaughter was sought after simply for being a white British child with blue eyes. I couldn't believe what I was hearing; it left me utterly stunned.

Holding my granddaughter for the last time and saying goodbye with my son was the most heartbreaking experience I have ever faced. We carry our broken hearts, but with each passing year, I feel we are getting closer to being reunited. I had never heard of forced adoptions until we went through this experience ourselves, but one day, I will share this story with the world.

Me changing my mindset got me and my son through the heartbreaking experience. When you change your mindset and reprogram your limiting beliefs, you approach challenges differently. I used to wonder why things were happening to me; now, I see them as opportunities for growth and progress. This journey is about learning, evolving, and making the right choices to become a better version of yourself and to shape a brighter future.

We all have choices, and making the right ones can be transformative. I left school at 15 with no GCSE's and had my first son at 17, my journey was full of ups and downs due to the wrong choices that I had made. But once I started my personal development journey and started making the right choices everything changed.

I take pride in all I've overcome and the empowered woman I am today, living a life I once thought was unattainable for someone like me. I've created my dream life, and one of my long-held aspirations has always been to help others. Now, I do that every day, finding immense fulfilment in watching other women turn their pain into power and embrace life's journey and manifest the life they desire.

Everything in my life—both the good and the bad—I have manifested. Now that I'm in complete alignment, I effortlessly manifest my dreams. I cleared my £20,000 debt, built successful businesses, and live in abundance and harmony. I've also attracted a balanced relationship filled with love, laughter, and happiness, with a partner who supports me as I support him.

My sons have a mother they can be proud of, and I take pride in myself as well, I've made my family proud. I once felt like a nobody, lacking belief in myself and my dreams, burdened by guilt over past mistakes. I no longer refer to them as mistakes, I call them lessons. When you learn from them, you grow. By choosing to heal internally, we also heal our children, as we serve as their mentors.

In my online manifesting academy, I cover everything needed to heal from within, completely transform your life, and create a better version of yourself while manifesting the life you deserve and desire. It also includes accredited energy healing courses for each member. It's not just a job for me, it's my passion and my life, and I absolutely love the impact the VIP Manifesting Academy has had on so many women.

Not only have all the women in the VIP program transformed their lives, but I've also had around one hundred ladies successfully come off meditation and antidepressants. The mindset is the most powerful tool we possess, and when you apply the right techniques to change it, you can completely transform your world

One of the reasons I established my academy was to ensure that many people could access healing sessions and mentorship, which they might not be able to afford otherwise. I wanted to create a safe space for women at an affordable price, allowing them to stay committed to their journeys.

The Souls and Spirit magazine called me the "Manifesting Guru," and some refer to me as the "Mindset Queen." However, I prefer to think of myself as the mentor who makes a difference. I genuinely care about each of my VIP members and want to see them succeed in their lives. Witnessing their transformations is the most rewarding feeling, and I am there for them every step of the way—cheering them on as their biggest supporter. The academy is like a soul family comprised of women at various stages of their journeys, all working towards becoming the best versions of themselves and creating their dream lives.

Get In Touch

If you would like to start your development and manifesting journey you can connect with me via Facebook at: Gemma Elizabeth Williams at **https://www.facebook.com/manifestingguru8**

Join the VIP manifesting academy at **www.manifestinggurus.com**

Join my free Facebook Group **"Empowerher Manifesting Mentor."**

You can find me on Instagram **@empowerher_mentor**

My YouTube channel is **EmpowerHer888**

You can also message me directly for a free one to one call to discuss how the academy can help you.

Some Thank You's

I would like to thank my sons for teaching me what real love is, for teaching me many different lessons. For giving me a reason to create a better version of myself and future for us all.

My partner for believing in me and my dreams.

My mum, stepdad, sister and brother for loving me unconditionally.

My Nan and Grandad for guiding me.

My spirit guides and Angels and God for never giving up on me, I love you all.

I would also like to say to all the ladies in my VIP Manifesting Academy. I am so proud of each and every one of you, for starting your journey. I believe in you and the best is yet to come!

Chapter Two

By Rachel Harper

Introduction

Watching my dad collapse in agony right in front of me as a five-year-old was terrifying. One moment, I was just going to kiss him goodnight; the next, he was writhing on the floor in unbearable pain. It's one of my earliest memories—so vivid, yet I had no idea how much it would shape my future. Did that moment alter the course of my life? Did the beliefs I formed back then—"It's all my fault, I am useless"—pave the way for the chaos that followed? Maybe. Maybe not. But it was the first of many horrific experiences that left deep imprints on me.

Now, at 48, a single mother, I've carried decades of addiction, worthlessness, and betrayal. But I'm writing this not as a victim, but as someone who broke free. I've survived violent relationships, rape, attempted murder, and some very close calls with suicide. For years, I functioned as a lost little girl, desperate to be loved, to feel safe, to hear someone say, "It's going to be okay." But no one ever did. So, I had to learn to say it to myself. This is my story. Not just of the darkness, but of how I clawed my way back to the light.

Early Struggles And An Absent Mind

Mum and dad split when I was six years old, and I was then met with the decision of who I wanted to live with. A choice I never thought would be asked of me, but the decision had already been made by all accounts. Every other weekend, Dad took me to theme parks and fun places. Then suddenly, he disappeared. I was just seven, I think. The next thing I know I was on a plane to Malaga to visit him for two weeks. I was only eight years old, and I flew on my own with a chaperone.

I came home, and that was the last I saw of him until I was maybe 12. I bumped into him walking along the street one day. He said hello, gave me some money and a hug and then left!

I was stoned up to my eyeballs at that point, and it was a really surreal situation. I was already being bullied at school for having blonde curly hair and awful baby pink national health glasses. I went by the name of Goldilocks and four eyes. I didn't have the support from both parents and I certainly never felt like anybody was fighting my battles for me and so I never said anything to anybody. My mother only grew suspicious when I was feeling sick every day before school. The fear of going in was unbearable. So eventually I moved schools and made some new friends, but I was never invited round for sleepovers, you know the PJ and pillow fight type of girl parties.

My mum was always at work and had a job in a pub and a nightclub on top of her daytime job, as Dad never paid a penny of maintenance for me. So, I sought affection with a group of friends who offered a strong bond and connection. Heavy metal music, spliffs and White Lightning were on the menu most nights. It was good for a few years until the effects of the drugs had consequences for some in the group. Drug psychosis and the suicide of one of our friends, Carl, at just 24, was an enormous shock. He'd come round to visit on my mum's birthday. I was the last person to see him alive before he drove off to the nearby car park and fumigated the car. I'm not sure where exactly I put those feelings until later on in life.

By now I was 14 and had a boyfriend, young I know, but we were very close. There was a pregnancy which, as a young child myself, I took the decision to terminate as there was no chance I felt capable of having a baby myself. After a while, Chris became increasingly possessive and violent towards me. There were several occasions of entrapment, coercive, and malicious behaviour and comments. On the way home along an alleyway he would make remarks like "there's no point you looking behind because they'll get you from the front" or "no matter where you go I will always find you." Over the course of our two-year relationship, he had manipulated me in such a way that I was completely brainwashed and susceptible to his behaviour. I suppose, looking back, he was a narcissist, but I was too young to realize.

The Beginning Of The End

As the purple smoke filled the car and I began to lose my senses, the sound of Nirvana's song "come as you are" on the radio got quieter and quieter. I remember thinking, "I'm not going to let this bastard be the one that ends my life!" Little did I know I was already on the verge of becoming unconscious. He made me sit on the back seat and he clasped my hands as he told me to breathe in deeply. I would try to cipher the fumes between my teeth, making it sound like I was inhaling a lot, but in fact, I was trying to ingest as little as possible. As the car filled with plumes of carbon monoxide, the last thought I had was a feeling of determination and that I must survive, because if I don't, my mum will kill me. How ironic. I came round, after how long I don't know, but the car had cut out!! He was sat on the back seat next to me out cold. I immediately thought, "I need to get the fuck out of this car and run!!"

It was pitch black and I was in the middle of a field—one sock on, no t-shirt, disoriented. He'd used these to plug the exhaust pipe and the gap in the window where the hose pipe came through. It later turned out we were in the middle of a pig field, hence the strange noise.

I got out and stood by the car, and sucked in the fresh night air. It was mid-March and still quite cold. As I contemplated running to God knows where, as I had no idea where the nearest house was, I began to think "what if he comes round and starts chasing me, I'd be dead for sure!" He'd stab me with the carving knife he had taken from my mum's kitchen. He'd broken into our family home earlier that day and was waiting for me to come home from school. It was at this point he met me at the bottom of the stairs with the knife covered in blood. Our lodger had come home before me. He bound and gagged her upstairs in my bedroom. He then took me to her car at knifepoint and stole it. We then drove miles. He was extremely erratic and threatened to throw me off the Orwell Bridge. We were missing for 9 hours and had both Norfolk and Suffolk Police looking for us.

By now, my conscience had kicked in. I couldn't leave him to die and so I opened the car door and shook him until he came round. The next few hours were ultimately just as harrowing as the experience itself. We drove to a petrol station where he filled up and then drove off, eventually stopping a further 13 miles down the road with armed police surrounding the car shouting and pointing guns at us. He was arrested and I was taken straight to the police house opposite Heath Road hospital. There I had to stand on a brown paper sheet and undress item by item, with each being placed into plastic evidence bags. I also had to have a full examination including an internal. In a plea for him not to fumigate the car, I agreed to sex. I was petrified and only consented in order to save my life. This constituted rape in the eyes of the law, and it certainly felt like it.

After the examination I was driven back to the police station where I was reunited with my mum, this was a very strange experience. As she waited in the interview room and the door opened, it seemed like ages before she came running over to give me a cuddle. It certainly didn't feel like any joy or relief or arms were being thrown around me. There were a few minutes of silence, disbelief, and a kind of awkwardness in the air. I felt so alone, and it was only then that I realised how much our mother and daughter relationship had broken down and been damaged.

A severe breakdown of communication over the years, not feeling like I had any purpose, direction or guidance, had led me to become unapproachable, and disrespectful, with no respect for myself or others. I'd say I had kind of shut down, but it was more like "let's just get fucked up". While I was lost inside my own head, I'll never have to deal with these emotions.

Losing Myself To Addiction And Despair

Every time I moved, whether it be jobs, places, friendship groups or even countries, I'd always end up falling into the same functioning mess that I was so used to. The drink, the drugs, the pubs, the clubs, the lock-ins, the kitchens, it never bloody stopped! The jobs, oh I've had so many jobs, and to be honest, I was a model employee. But really, I was just a functioning bundle of erratic emotions that would bounce from one place to another, leaving a trail of destruction behind me. Failed relationships, failed jobs and generally failing in life. I felt so fucking lost inside, but to the outside world I was this lovely, lively, bubbly, gregarious blonde haired bombshell with a great personality. I was having the time of my life, so they thought. But really, I was just chasing the feeling of being loved, feeling special, admired, included, being heard and appreciated.

I was crying out for help because the cocaine addiction had taken hold and I was registered alcohol dependent. The intent to just get so wasted and be so detached from myself while remaining functional, funny, assertive and, I suppose, noticed, was my main purpose. I had no drive, no desire and nothing to look forward to or to really focus on. Suicidal thoughts were rife, and on several occasions, it was attempted. Thankfully, I was either caught in time or I came to my senses and thought I deserve better than this.

This Is It

For years, I told myself, "This is it. This is who I am. There's no changing it." Thirty-four years of addiction. How do you undo a lifetime of self-destruction? Then, in October 2017, I found out I was pregnant. Due to my lifestyle, several abortions and miscarriage, I presumed myself baron. However, Billy had other ideas. And he has once said to me "mummy I chose you". My Spirit guides had again got other ideas for me. I was met with surprise, excitement, but huge amounts of fear and trepidation. I was still drinking, still using, and the doctors warned me not to stop cold turkey or my body could go into shock. But for the first time in my life, I had something bigger than my demons. Billy.

I had my son in June 2018 and life was good, however the relationship with his father was not, and after feeling so exceptionally lucky and gifted to have been given this chance of being a mother I found myself thinking, "I have to do this on my own, because I haven't got the capacity to be in a relationship and be a mother at the same time." I wouldn't have coped…and to be honest, I wasn't. Dealing with the cold turkey of coming off drugs, stopping drinking, facing emotions I'd suppressed for so long, being a mum and a partner was too much. Something had to give.

So I did the hardest thing I've ever done. I made the decision to leave as I needed space and to do it my own way, no distractions. I then found myself on my own with a one-and-a-half-year-old son and a cat. Everything I'd ever wished for in all honesty. But it was tough. The feelings of "I'm not good enough" and "I don't deserve to have this loving child, and a life of happiness", were on occasions too much. It was at this point I had a breakdown, and I knew that little boy needed his mummy and his mummy needed to sort her fucking life out and step into that person that she should have always been.

Turning Point

I discovered a modality called Belief coding founded by Jessica Cunningham, and I went away for three days to Sheffield where I experienced a kind of therapy that I had never had before. I went on to train as a Belief Coding Facilitator, and as part of my accreditation I would have to perform sessions on myself, a skill I still use today. Over the next few years, I found myself on a journey travelling through time, quantum fields, astrological storms, mind bending experiences and finally coming to rest in a place where calm and focus ensues, and the ability to manifest my dreams and desires is now a path of purpose and excitement.

Finding Freedom And Releasing The Past

Breaking free from the clutches of cocaine and alcohol for so long was no mean feat. However, the freedom, the clarity, the focus and determination, the zest for life, the ability to learn and retain information, the discovery of so many new people and topics, and stepping back into something and someone that I used to be have been truly liberating. However, at times, it has been so lonely. But this was a path that needed to be taken and I have definitely learnt from this experience.

From this point two years ago, I have embarked on a journey that can only be described as like sitting on a roller coaster ride, whizzing up and down, round and round, and being thrown around in an emotional ball of anger, hatred, resentment, fear and hope, but I eventually found the source of what lights me up as a child, subjects on the mind, the art world and AI, and also my ability to laugh naturally, feel content, be unique and step into my intuitive authentic self.

This lets me shine my light again after it was dimmed for so long.

Stepping Into Purpose

I now focus my time on being the best possible Mum I can be. I educate myself daily with personal growth and self-development topics, understanding human behaviour and human design, Ancestral trauma, future self and inner freedom techniques, coaching others and helping those who have spent a life of feeling like they're just not worth it, it's not worth trying and what's the fucking point! I understand how people so easily step into this lifelong cycle however, my walls have been built so high that I struggle to tolerate those who talk and moan about a situation but do fuck all to change it.

I know how difficult it is and I believe in you. You too can do it too!! I fought so hard to get out of my predicaments on so many occasions and boy did I fucking try. I was once refused help because "I wasn't bad enough, because I functioned." So, when you have tried to pick yourself up time and time and time again, and then finally and thankfully, that last nail never got hit in that coffin, you rise above and beyond a level you never thought possible, to find another layer of haters and doubters, people ready to knock you back down, drag you back into that same circle because they are stuck there themselves. I believe so many are longing to get out of that pond. But you've got to really, really want to do it. That switch can click at any moment in time, and you never know what is around the corner.

Conclusion And Takeaway

I have lived a very colourful life and there are other instances of rape, violent and abusive relationships and near-death experiences that I could share, but on the whole, there has been a magnitude of laughter, excitement, adventure and generally not knowing what the fuck is going to happen next. I now live my life feeling that it's not the end, it's actually just beginning. And as a manifesting generator, I flip from one thing to another and have several different and exciting opportunities on the go. Offering an array of unique experiences to help guide those in need and on their very own path to freedom.

I feel watching my dad have that heart attack although those years ago, and generally the men closest to me fucking me over one way or another, (there's another story about that but my word count is almost at its capacity) my life has possibly gone full circle. I was so innocent and so loved to then feel so alone and isolated to then having so much resentment and hatred, I would push people away so as not to feel hurt, but I've learned how to forgive and let live. Now I smile and the world smiles back at me. So now I'm living a fairly simple life, I still enjoy being very dynamic in what I do, how I help people and the different opportunities I present. Life really is like a box of chocolates, and everyone is different. So am I. And I'm definitely not a one size fits all person.

So, if you feel called, please head over to my Facebook profile where things can get a bit real and raw, you will also find all my other links to other interests I have and products/services I enjoy and opportunities where I will personally guide you to possibly a life towards your dreams.

My group Riiize to the Freedom Revolution also has exciting information and details of how the world is changing… for the better, and we can be part of it. If you aren't on socials, please email me at **Riiizewithrachel@gmail.com**

Thank you for taking the time to hear just a snippet of my story. I hope it has given someone the inspiration to make that change and believe that good things can come to you if you really, really want it.

Take good care

One love

Chapter Three

By Sian Taylor

Build Up To Burnout And Beyond

Four years ago, I reached burnout and my life as I knew it imploded. Recovery in itself was enough but what I didn't know was that the core relationships in my life, the ones which I thought were constant, were about to unravel. I had no choice but to surrender into the cycles of the abyss as time went on. From the beginning I had a sense that all would become clear and that there was a higher purpose for all this, but didn't think it would take as long, what else lay in store and that it would be as challenging and painful as it has been.

This is not going to be one of those 'I was a mess and now I have the golden solution' stories. I have been a mess, and life continues to provide its challenges. I mean, honestly, whose doesn't?! This is a condensed account of survival in the face of persistent chronic stress, made up of multi-layered events and interwoven threads. Some of the events I talk about are very much current at the time of writing. I hope that this will reach out and resonate with anyone going through something similar. We women are incredibly strong and can forget that in the firefighting of our lives!

The Beginning Of The Unravelling

At the beginning of 2021 I was working in, what, on the face of it was an appropriate job for me, as a support worker with a local housing charity, as well as working a few late shifts in their night shelter. My early dreams of a career working in theatre had long been abandoned through the need for survival. I had a partner of six years. My children, who I had battled to raise as a single parent against many stacking odds, were grown, and functioning independently in their chosen areas of work. I had, so I thought at the time, come to forgive myself for not having been able to be the parent I had wanted to be.

The key moment when everything as I knew it began to implode was February of that year. I'd had my six-month review in my job and passed with flying colours, so I should have been flying high, but instead, I was exhausted. No – beyond exhausted. Exhausted to a degree I had not experienced before. There were money worries, debts, pressures from all sides, juggling expectations and tensions between those closest to me. The pandemic had been ongoing for a year and society was crumbling all around through fearmongering and division. I decided to book a week's leave at the end of the month for some rest. Previously in my life when I'd hit exhaustion point, I used to know that three days bed rest would sort it – one to sleep, one to rest and the third to recover. At the end of the week, however, I felt no better. My limbs felt so heavy. I couldn't concentrate to read anything, not even messages on my phone let alone process and respond to them. I couldn't even follow a simple TV programme. It was like being an alien having landed on a strange planet. As the week went on, I felt a rising sense of panic, like I was on a train steaming ahead to certain doom and I was desperately clawing backwards. I knew this was something I couldn't just push through and repeatedly my inner dialogue was screaming 'I can't do it anymore!!' and yet I had no idea what 'it' was. I no longer had the strength to carry the weight of the expectations and responsibilities of my adult life and just had to relinquish and let go.

Scratch the surface, though, and it begins to be clear to see. I was under pressure from all directions. I was working one full time job in the day, part-time at night, and had hands-on involvement in my partner's business. The earnings from my job covered just the household bills, no more, and so as a result we were reliant on the inconsistency of what came in from the business. The dynamic of the relationship wasn't healthy. I was engaged in network marketing. I was supporting my daughter who had recently given birth to her second baby. It seemed like I was frequently in the middle of conflicts between family members.

I was also living up to other people's expectations, both real and perceived, ignoring myself and putting others needs ahead of mine for an easier, quieter life. I had also been, I've come to realise, masking from undiagnosed ADHD and/or CPTSD and hitting perimenopause; my body simply couldn't push through as it had up until then.

Before The Before

The path of least resistance on the outside meant destroying and suppressing myself on the inside, and I'd been doing this for so many years that I didn't know how to be any different. Having been raised to be a good girl, suppressing certain parts of myself it was easier to mask, avoid disappointing or creating conflict, not expressing myself fully.

When I was 17, I met the toxic individual who had a huge and lasting impact on my life. He was 2 years older than me, had already left school, wore leathers for going on his motorcycle and seemed so cool to me. There was me, a naïve, young sixth-former from an all-girls school who spent her time avoiding homework, and going to dance and drama lessons, performing in shows, and partying with friends at the weekends. Looking back now, I can see all the classic stages, starting with love bombing, an incident which I'd buried and only recently have recognised as rape, lies, infidelity, which was always somehow my fault, his alcoholism, broken promises, gaslighting and so on - all of which have had a lasting impact on my psyche.

The Journey

The relationship lasted eight years, during which time I married and had children with him. For many years after the divorce, he continued to have a stronghold over me. That stronghold was my most vulnerable spot, which was my love for the children, maintaining his control through and around them. I was living in constant fear that he would take the children as he was always claiming that he was a better parent. He never did, of course, but that threat was implicit. It took years to realise it was all about controlling me and manipulating rather than doing what was best for the children.

I became divorced with two children at the age of 27 and felt ashamed, bewildered and a failure. My confidence was shattered, I was estranged from friends and emotionally disconnected from family. It took about two years, I think, before I was able to join the dots and put the word abuse to the relationship. Nowadays we have the term coercive control.

The single mum years became both the most challenging and joyous times. Challenging because I was constantly battling the negative influence of my ex whilst living in fear as he pulled the strings of the psychological control he had embedded in our years together. Joyous because it was a time of purpose, providing for the children who were my reason for getting up in those mornings where I didn't feel like it (and there were many). I found inner strength I wasn't aware I had. There was a constant tiredness which looking back I realise was depression. I went back to studying and achieved a first-class honours degree. I was attuned to Reiki levels 1 and 2 and was actively involved on the committees of the pre-school and then school. There were holidays in France with my parents, the support of extended family and a good group of single mum friends who all helped each other out. I learned independence, and although I occasionally wondered what it might be like to be with someone, I loved the peace of the evenings when the children were in bed, and I could do as I pleased. I turned thirty, passed my driving test and graduated in the same year.

In 2006, I decided to move myself and the children to Wales where I thought they would have a better chance of growing up at their own pace. We would be closer to my family and roots, and I could continue my studies.

Around the period the marriage broke down, aged three, my son had started with violent meltdowns. As time went on, I took the blame for what was happening, believing that it must be my fault somehow, and terrified that if my ex knew he would have the children taken away, using this as an example of what a bad parent I was. At a chance encounter when my son was around fourteen, I was told about Pathological Demand Avoidance and the behaviour seemed to fit. The approaches I had been taking intuitively and which worked, tallied with how to cope with it. While he was acting out and getting most of the attention, my daughter quietly withdrew and took the stress out on herself, which only came to light later in her teen years.

In the face of all of this, I was working part-time, took on a part-time PGCE as well as a part-time Masters. By the end of the first term, I started to see how all the busy-ness was really a way of avoiding what was bubbling underneath, a trauma response. I dropped the PGCE, and I took my son out of school to Home Educate, which helped ease the pressure in the household.

In 2013, I had a spiritual rebirth with the Light of Love. It helped release self-judgement, and the need to understand everything, which was a huge step forward.

During Burnout

Gradually, tentatively, in those first few months, I had no option but to go back to basics in terms of self-care and daily routines, consciously recognising when I was reaching my limits. For someone who had spent most of her adult life powering through, it was a shock to not be able to do that any longer. I went through cycles of deep depression, suicidal ideation, agoraphobia, paranoia, and guilt. I was scared that I would never get better, trying to figure out what was causing this deep tiredness I could feel in my body.

A year on from hitting that wall, unwanted feelings rose to the surface. I remember sitting on the floor of my daughter's living room with her beautiful baby and toddler, in that house full of love and pure joy, and a feeling of sadness rising within me. At first, I could not understand where it was coming from or what it was about, then I realised that somehow the echo of how I had felt when my children were that small had come back. I made the difficult decision to step back while I processed it. This resulted in a chain of misunderstandings and hurt with my daughter, which resulted in an estrangement of eighteen months. The circumstances over which we started speaking again were even more earth shattering.

In March of 2021, my son delivered me an ultimatum. In that moment I saw echoes of the past, as if his father were standing in front of me – only this time, I could see the tactics and so I didn't acquiesce to his demand. I knew, as his mother, for both our sakes, I had to lay that boundary down. He left and moved in with his sister. A few weeks later, after more misunderstandings, both children cut me out. It was utterly devastating. This triggered me back into paranoia of the discard phase of the relationship with their father, when I was questioning deeply whether it was me who was the narcissist after all, and the suicidal thoughts came back. I had to go through a painful grieving process of letting go of the idea that I had been a good, though flawed, mother, and the identity I had built in my adult life. I knew this was the time to discover who I really was without them.

The failing business then went bankrupt. My partner and I gave up our shop and flat and started on van life, leaving the town where the children were. For the first time in years, I felt free. This feeling was short-lived as the realities of living hand to mouth in a trade that didn't fill me with joy brought out the feeling of being trapped again.

The Gift That Keeps On Giving

Eighteen months after the heartbreak of the separation from the children and grandchildren, an event brought my daughter and I back in contact. My son had been arrested at her house, which was hugely traumatic for her. Until then, she would have fought to the ends of the earth for her brother. What followed with him cracked open the relationship which has allowed for more light and healing to enter for us.

Four months after finding out about my son's arrest, and 25 years to the day since giving birth to him, I was in the same hospital with my parents whilst my mother's terminal diagnosis was confirmed. The rest of 2023 was spent being with her, caring and nursing as she declined. It was a harrowing and precious time for which I will be eternally grateful.

During those long months, as the pressure mounted, further cracks appeared even closer to home. I am the middle of three daughters, and the idea was that we would share the caring as much as we could. I positioned myself to be there the most as my circumstances were the most flexible. Wild horses would have had to prevent me from being there anyway! What really became apparent in this period of mounting stress and pressure was that we weren't quite the collaborative team I had thought. Things really came to a head on Mam's death day when one sister created a huge drama, taking the focus away from our Mam and on to her.

In the background, the pressures within my relationship had been mounting and I felt trapped and powerless. I had no income of my own and did not want to add to the worry for my family, so I stayed, trying to make the best of it. Looking back, neither of us was happy and the stress levels were so high. 'Van life' had become 'caravan in a friend's field life' which was better in some ways, but it was clear that we weren't building any foundations as things were. I wasn't living life, merely existing, and I was operating within small parameters. Many years ago, a homeopath had said to me that I was like a bird sitting in a cage with the door open and its only now I'm starting to understand. I have jumped from cage to cage feeling trapped and wishing for freedom when freedom was out there all along. At the end of July last year, just after being attuned to the pink rose energy, there was one last straw, and I stepped out of that situation.

Three weeks later, exactly eight months after Mam's funeral, and the night after a lovely twenty-four hours with him, my Dad passed away suddenly. His heart had been weakening since Mam's passing and he was becoming increasingly frail but even so, the shock and devastation were totally overwhelming. Dad was my rock, my companion, and he and Mam had been our biggest supporters. Wherever they were was always home. Losing them both within such a short space of time has been huge. Suddenly, the family I'd thought of as strong and healthy until a few months before, was reduced in numbers, not just from the loss of Mam and Dad, but the estrangement from my son and a sister. Now, we were grieving, in shock and trying to act in our father's interests with the dawning realisation that the toxic dynamics we were battling with had been going on for most of our lives.

Now

During the months of my mother's last illness, driven by the motivation of planning beyond the ending we knew was coming, I trained as a Life Coach. I felt it was important to show her that I was headed in a direction professionally and for me, looking ahead to something positive for after. I learned so much and it opened my eyes to view dynamics within the family with different eyes and understand what was going on. I could see situations and reactions of others from a more detached place without automatically feeling that it must be my fault somehow.

I have also been attuned to more Energy Healing modalities, which I offer in-person and online, and love witnessing the positive effects of healing energies on clients. This is also the year I turn fifty. My family is smaller but lighter and healthier. My daughter and I have rebuilt a loving and respectful relationship. I am proud of the woman she has become, and how she and her partner parent their daughters. I have bonded with my granddaughters who I adore, who bring infinite joy and brighten up any room.

I have a deeper appreciation of this life and how short and precious it is. I have started working as a mentor for Autistic and ADHD students supporting them through university and am loving it! I get paid to be me, using my coaching skills where appropriate and its doing wonders for my self-esteem, to have an income again and a sense of being of value. Soon, I aim to train more deeply on how to support others in working through and releasing trauma with the longer term goal of providing sanctuary for women needing respite from their everyday lives.

If you would like to connect with me, you can find me here: **https://linktr.ee/findingfreedom2_**

Chapter Four

By Helen Stephens

This Is Me

Hello everyone, I'm Helen, a 40-year-old married mum to 2 beautiful children and a little fur baby dog. I'm very pleased to meet you and I'm so excited to be writing a chapter in this book! I'm just a regular woman, who is trying to find her way in the world and live out my passions in the process. I've grown, made mistakes, learnt from them, am trying to figure out my end goal and of course manifest my dreams!

I would say that my curiosity and interest in all things spiritual has grown on me and has become an important part of my life. It fascinates me to think that the world has been programmed to always think inside the box and once you understand the magic, then you can truly grow and achieve anything!

Ever since I was born, I have loved animals and had lots of different pets. I enjoy being creative through artwork, catching up with friends and having lots of fun. I would say that my ways have changed, obviously as I've grown, learnt more and I suffered a brain injury, which I will tell you more about later on. When social media, especially Facebook came into existence, it allowed me to explore, learn, strengthen my spiritual love and connect with people from all over the world! I have admired the spiritual side and all of its elements for some time; hence why I undertook my Reiki training.

I'm also a massive fan of crystals and I have a house full of them! Their meanings fascinate me, and I find them so beautiful. I love all things witchy, magical and do cast the odd spell now and again.

My mum was born with a connection to the other realm, and I am always fascinated by her stories. I embraced this and I've been delighted by my ability to pick fantastic messages for myself from my tarot deck and I've even manifested a raffle win! I have learnt and do continue to learn a lot about manifestation and I'm always trying to strengthen my mindset and positivity.

My own business is that I carry out Tarot readings with my Green Witch deck and I also give Reiki treatments. What's Reiki? you may ask, well it's related to energy healing. The practitioner acts as a funnel for universal light to be sent to the client through the practitioner's hands. I find it very exciting and am passionate about helping people to feel better within themselves. I'm still in the early stages of growing my business, which brings me so much joy and pleasure. I love all things girly, health and wellbeing products and have incorporated this into my business as well.

I love being an influencer for an amazing brand that I've just partnered with, especially when you get to try out new products with amazing reviews, grab a fantastic bargain and share your experience with everyone! (I love sharing!). You can find out more from my Facebook page, which I've mentioned below. I love it as it all links in together with wellbeing and positivity.

I do feel that our head spaces can have a huge effect on our lives. If you're always thinking negatively or saying that bad things are going to happen, you are almost telling the universe that this is what you want. I am definitely a 'yes' for positive thinking! Like everyone I can find it hard at times especially when I'm tired and life can be tough. I love connecting with the earth and mother nature by lying on the grass and letting all my tension melt away, letting my body and mind relax. It's so important for our wellbeing to take time out for ourselves. It's also a great idea to write everything down that's on your mind and then burn the piece of paper so that you can release it and feel a little lighter.

I was very lucky to meet my now husband via internet dating, we have our 2 beautiful children and a dog. I love our house and think that we are very blessed to have what we have, thank you Universe. One huge thing that I definitely want to have ticked off my bucket list is to have my own horse one day as I've always loved them (definitely one on my manifesting list!).

In The Beginning, Hello World!

Looking back at my younger days I would say that I was full of zest for life, and I wanted to achieve. I wanted to get a job working with animals, but I didn't achieve a C in GCSE maths at school, so I wasn't too sure which way I was going to go or what I was going to do. Unfortunately, I can remember having a 'not enough' mindset in my teenage years, which I know is silly because I did have lots of lovely things such as family, friends, and a house to live in. I do hate the way that this world puts us at competition with each other and I turned to spiritual practices such as meditation and oracle cards to help get me out of this mindset. It's important to remember to take time out for ourselves. This might be going for a walk, taking a nice relaxing bath, having a Reiki session (!) or just doing something that you enjoy and find rewarding.

Growing up I would spend my weekends down at my local horse-riding stables helping out. I really enjoyed being active and getting to ride. Unfortunately, I decided to leave when I was about 13 as I am such a sensitive person and there were people who were making me feel very sad. I more often than not will flee instead of staying and fighting as I find 'out of sight out of mind' a more positive action step for my mental health.

After finishing secondary school, I went to college and didn't really study subjects that I was that passionate about. When I left college, I wasn't sure what I was going to do but I went on to university to study an equine degree, which I loved and made fantastic friendships from. The degree covered everything to do with horses. I was thinking about getting a job working with horses, but I wasn't too sure about which path I would go down. I did think about doing equine massage and that was something that I was going to do a bit of research on to find out more about. I think that alternate therapies are in my blood as I've always been interested in that path and feel passionate about it.

How One Event Can Change Your Whole Life

In 2006 I would say that my life changed forever as sadly I was involved in a horrific car crash whilst I was in my final year at university. I can't remember the crash as I was driving an old car that didn't have an airbag, so my head hit the steering wheel and my brain wiped the memory out. My friends were in a car behind me so they were first on the scene, and I can't imagine how it must have been for them to see me like that.

I was airlifted to hospital in a helicopter and my family had to drive all the way to the hospital where I was, not knowing how they would find me and it was very much touch and go. Thankfully I survived and I do have fond memories of being in hospital. It was strange coming round, and I think the first thought that I can vaguely remember was that I woke up and heard my mum's voice, so I knew that I was safe and it was ok to go back to sleep. It was almost like going back to being a child needing support and love to help me get better.

Three or four months later I was out of hospital and back at home, still alive and kicking (no pun intended). I was going to go back to university as well to complete my final year. I don't know how I picked myself back up again. My injuries to me made me look like a different person and I thought that person was ugly. I also had to learn to walk again as my thigh bone had shattered and an implant had been put into my leg, so I had to get used to walking on it.

My accident happened when I was 21 and I'm now 40. Living with a head injury can be difficult because on the outside you look the same as everyone else, but obviously inside my brain was damaged. I do worry about how I react sometimes to situations, but I usually find out that I'm blowing it out of proportion in my head. I've learnt that you're always harder on yourself than what others are thinking about you.

To this day I'm a shopaholic (you don't want to see how much make-up I have) and I always try to make myself look 'perfect' because of what I feel that I lost on that day. Sadly, I do almost feel like I'm trying to replace something, such as the way that I used to look by buying things but obviously that's never going to happen.

I know it sounds silly and unfortunately, I know that this world puts a huge emphasis on saying that you should look a certain way. I absolutely adore Katie Piper, and I think she is so amazing with her work, positivity and how she is finding ways to overcome her trauma. One step at a time I do feel that the world is changing its views, which is fantastic.

I also find it difficult to have a clear path and I almost feel like I'm figuring it out as I go along. It can sometimes feel like I know what I should be doing, but it seems like it's taking forever to get there. With finding my forever job I've found it difficult to fix on one thing and there have been obstacles blocking me. I have had plenty of minimum wage jobs that I seem to go through, I sometimes think that because of my head injury, does it mean that I get bored, and I can't stick? On the other hand, I need to really look within myself and do something that I am passionate about. I love Reiki and helping people, so that's why I naturally wanted to learn more and become qualified in it.

The Journey

I have also looked at jobs that you need to pay for the training so that you can become qualified in that field, and I usually don't have the money to spare. I have managed to pay for my Reiki training, which I really loved doing. I need to concentrate on getting my business out into the world as I feel that I have so much to give.

It is a bit strange as being self-employed keeps coming up for me (I think the universe may be trying to tell me something!), and as a Reiki practitioner that is what you become. It can also be difficult if you feel that you don't have support, but I love the fact that I have found supportive groups on Facebook. Remember never to doubt your dreams as they are yours and yours alone.

There are other spiritual tools that I enjoy using such as vision boards, incense, crystals, oracle and Tarot cards. There is so much that you can learn about, and I do find it fascinating. I became hooked on Reiki as when I had a treatment and was learning about the ancient art it felt so wonderful to me. I was able to relax and switch off from the busyness of the world and I really wanted to share it with others.

I found spirituality to be very therapeutic and people were coming together over social media who were all embracing this. I found so much on different social platforms, and this helped my curiosity to grow and for me wanting to start a business, as I feel gifted, and I love helping people. I just get a warm fuzzy feeling when I know that I've helped someone to feel better and stronger, plus it feels wonderful! I achieved my Reiki level 1, level 2 and angel Reiki in 2023 at Bedford with the fantastic Gemma Williams as my teacher. It was an amazing experience, and I loved every second of it.

I have a strong feeling that 2025 is going to be such a fantastic year so I really want to get my Reiki and Tarot reading out there so that I can really help and heal people. When I've done or been given a treatment, I feel so relaxed and much better with myself. When I give

Reiki treatments to others, I find it so enjoyable as I'm helping that person to heal.

I'm aligning myself with manifestation processes in particular such as knowing that words are spells and I'm always trying to say positive things. I dare you to try it friends, say to yourself 'It's so amazing that I found £5, how awesome is that' you may be pleasantly surprised and don't forget to believe in what you're saying as well!

The future… I would love to embrace and help as many people as I can with my spiritual ways such as giving Reiki treatments and Tarot card readings. I do feel a strong connection with animals, and I may also look at other treatments/help that I can offer. One career path that I have fairly recently looked at is to become a bridle fitter for horses. This would allow me to also connect with horses on a spiritual side as I would be helping them to have the best/comfortable bridle, which would benefit them through movement and mood. Again, as an empath I definitely feel that I can connect with living beings and am sensitive to their feelings. I do find it hard to cope with negativity but through working on myself spiritually I am becoming stronger.

One quote that I love is 'Always turn your face towards the sun and the shadows fall behind you.'

Life is definitely an adventure, and I would say from my experience that we do go through life stages. Living can be tough and that's why I want to share with you my alternative therapies so you can grab a piece of joy from the cake of life.

How I Can Help You

I carry out Reiki sessions either distantly or in person, to help you align your Chakra's so that you can shed your catalyst and shine like the beautiful butterfly that you are. Chakras are energy points in the body that can become blocked due to lifestyle and emotions, so it is very important to have these points cleansed and cleared.

I have a Facebook page called Helen's Curiosity Shop where I love to show and tell you all about the exciting things that I'm selling and can offer you. I also love giving out advice that might help someone such as getting them to buy a pack of positive Oracle cards. I would suggest that they pick one each day, read the message and carry the card with them so that they can feel positive.

I always enjoy following the moon cycles as I feel that they can make a real difference to us, what we are wanting to accomplish or how we want to feel in our lives. I love to share things like this on my Facebook page as well.

I am also massively into witchcraft with my witch's name being Raven Rose, I love casting spells and am definitely into manifesting. I always find that if you're feeling overloaded you should just grab a notebook and just put pen to paper and do a brain dump. It always helps me to feel lighter and then I can see if I need to take note of any action steps with what's been cluttering my mind. I also carry out Tarot card readings with my own Green Witch deck, which I have a fantastic connection to.

Where To Find Me And How To Connect

My page on Facebook is called Helen's Curiosity Shop where I regularly post items that I have for sale, tell people about my Reiki and I pull cards from my Tarot deck.

Here is the link to find my shop page: https://www.facebook.com/profile.php?id=61560150530098

Here is the link for my own Facebook profile: **https://www.facebook.com/helen.stephens111/**

You can contact me by email: **helen.stephens84@outlook.com**

We can discuss if you are interested in receiving healing through my Reiki, I can hold sessions with you online or in person. We can talk about any issues or problems that you may be facing if you wish, and I would set up a Reiki session for you. The sessions would be confidential, and you can have a free taster session first to see how you feel after the session and then we can discuss the next steps.

I do Tarot card readings, again online or in person. I love connecting on zoom for this so that we can have a chat, I can see you and you can see the cards when I carry out your reading.

It would be my pleasure to connect and to support you. I look forward to the future with hope, love and passion.

Chapter Five

By Sadie Hallett-Chambers

Sadie's Story – The Girl Behind The Mask

Introduction: The Call To Share My Story

Picture the scene: a cozy, autumnal Sunday evening, freshly emerged from a ritual goddess bath, feeling cleansed and rejuvenated. Wrapped in my comfiest pyjamas, candles flickering, incense lit, and a steaming cup of hot chocolate in hand, ready to tune into the 8pm weekly VIP Manifesting Academy workshop, hosted by the incredible Gemma Williams.

The energy in the session felt electric, even more high vibe than usual. Gemma had just made an exciting announcement: she was launching a co-author book collaboration and was looking for women with inspirational stories to take part. As I sat there, my mind began flicking through the chapters of my life the trials, the triumphs, the moments of despair and resilience. I had countless stories I could share… but one in particular burned brightly in my mind, demanding to be told. My survival story. Surviving COVID at the start of 2020.

Even though I had long felt this story needed to be shared, the thought of opening up so vulnerably and laying it all out for the world to see, felt daunting. Could I do that? Would people even want to read about a virus that, at the time, some refused to acknowledge even existed? The doubts and fears swirled around, after all, it has taken a lot of healing to get to where I am now. But deep down, I knew I wanted to share my journey in order to inspire others. So, before I could talk myself out of it, I signed there and then on the dotted line.

It's funny how life can shift in the blink of an eye. Five years ago, my Sunday nights looked very different. I'd be caught in the usual manic rush of prepping school stuff for the week, packing lunches for my full-time job as a mental health nurse. No goddess baths. No meditations. No sacred rituals. Self-care wasn't even a concept to me back then. Life felt like a never-ending cycle of organised (or rather, disorganized) chaos. Constantly moving from one thing to the next, with no space to pause, reflect, or breathe. No high-vibe tribe to uplift me, and certainly no VIP Academy.

The Academy changed so much for me. It helped shift my mindset, my energy, my entire life. And I wouldn't have found it had I not experienced my spiritual awakening in 2020. But what even is a spiritual awakening? I suppose it's different for everyone, yet a common theme seems to emerge which is that it often arises from the ashes of hitting rock bottom, from moments of desperation, from the aching need for something more. It's that glimmer of hope we cling to when we're lost in the dark.

The chapter you're about to read is my own story of fighting my way through that darkness, my journey of survival, and the profound transformation that followed. This is the story of the girl behind the mask.

That Fateful Day

"Do you really need to drive all the way up just to tell them you need to work from home?" If only I had listened to that sentence, the concern in my partner's voice. If only I could go back in time. I had no idea that this would be the work meeting that would change my life forever. Let's go back to mid-March 2020. It was an average early spring morning, nothing unusual about it. The 40-minute commute to work felt routine, just another day.

The Journey

I arrived at the office expecting a standard team meeting: another gathering in a familiar room, chairs arranged in a circle, occupied by clinicians, the team manager, and admin staff ready to take notes. But this meeting would be different. A word hung in the air, heavy, unfamiliar, a foreign invader laced with uncertainty-COVID-19. A virus we weren't yet ready to grasp in its full, devastating reality.

The purpose of the meeting was clear: as a mental health team, we needed to navigate how COVID would impact our work, our patients, and our roles as clinicians. I sat there, deep in thought. As a newly qualified mental health nurse, I was only just finding my feet in a career I loved, a career built on my lifelong passion for helping people. I had seen COVID on the news, but did I truly understand the severity? Naively, no, I didn't.

The meeting followed a structured plan. Those of us with weakened immune systems were asked to speak privately with the manager to discuss the possibility of working from home. I knew I fell into that category as due to having an autoimmune disease, I was at risk. So, I waited my turn, sitting through the discussion until a persistent, hacking cough filled the room. COUGH! COUGH! COUGH!

It came from the staff member sitting right next to me. We all noticed it. The sound cut through the air, impossible to ignore. Then, casually, flippantly, she uttered a sentence that is now etched into my mind forever: "Oh, I think I may have that COVID." In that moment, my fate was sealed. I had just unknowingly inhaled a high viral load of a new and deadly virus. My nightmare was only just beginning.

I've often sat and wondered: What if I had sat further away? What if she had called in sick that morning? What if I had just attended the meeting from home via zoom instead, like my partner had suggested? But isn't hindsight a wonderful thing? Since my spiritual awakening, I understand something I couldn't see before. We are all living out our own divine conversations, each moment unfolding as it is meant to, and as much as I once wished I could go back and change that day, this was always meant to be part of my journey.

Masks

The nurse shook her head. I could sense pity verging on doom as I locked eyes with hers, peering out from above the mask that hid the rest of her face. "Nope," she said, her voice firm yet laced with regret. "It's not helping." My heart pounded more in my chest. I had arrived at the last chance saloon, strapped to a CPAP machine—a Continuous Positive Airway Pressure device designed to force air into my failing lungs. It was a desperate attempt to keep me breathing, to prevent my body from shutting down completely.

Just twenty-four hours earlier, I had been at home, gasping for air but stubbornly refusing medical intervention. I had spent the past four days feeling unwell: body aches, a relentless cough, a rattling sensation in my chest at night. It felt like a bad chest infection, nothing more. I told myself I'd be fine. But I wasn't fine. It had taken me nearly ten minutes just to make it downstairs. When my partner saw me, pale faced, and lips tinged blue, he told me he was calling an ambulance. I wanted to protest, but I couldn't get enough air to argue. The next thing I knew, I was being rushed to the hospital, although my memory of the journey is hazy at best.

What I do remember is that on arrival a growing team of medical professionals surrounded me, their faces fixed with concern. I could hear the rhythmic beeping of monitors, see the gloved hands working quickly to insert IV lines. A nurse struggled to find a vein while another fitted an oxygen mask over my face.

Even then, I knew things were bad. I just didn't realise how bad.

"Fluffy globules covering my lungs." That was all I managed to type in a message to my partner, Jake, as I was switched to my second oxygen tank. A chest X-ray had just been taken, and the consultant explained that my lungs were riddled with COVID molecules—what he described as "fluffy globules." But I couldn't process what that meant.

My brain latched onto just one sentence. "We're calling ICU. Oxygen isn't reaching your bloodstream. We're really concerned." Thus, here I was now twenty-four hours later, and hooked up to a CPAP machine at its maximum setting yet it still wasn't working. My oxygen levels kept dropping. My body was starved of oxygen, and I was experiencing hypoxia. The sensation was terrifying it was if I was drowning. In reality, I was dying. Then came the words that hit me like a hammer to the skull: "You will have to be placed into a coma and onto a ventilator for any chance of survival."

For a moment, time seemed to freeze, but then something inside me ignited. This was not goodbye; I refused to let that be a thought. My body might be failing me, but my heart and spirit would not. I had two boys waiting for me at home and there was no way I would leave them without a Mum!

The Double D's, Darkness And Delirium

I have no memory of being put into the coma. My last recollection was hearing the words "lack of oxygen to the brain" and now, here I was face down, strapped to a wooden board, being wheeled around. I tried to speak. Nothing. I tried to move. Total paralysis. However, I could still hear. My hearing remained untouched, a cruel irony in what felt like a living nightmare. I listened intently, picking up voices-carers? So, this is it, then? My new reality? Trapped inside my own body, unable to move, unable to communicate. A vegetative state, with only my mind racing, screaming, begging to be heard.

If only they would turn me over. Why was I face down? All I could see were shoes. Endless shoes, passing in and out of my field of vision. If I could just see a face, maybe I could find a way to communicate. But the days stretched on, my only connection to the world the cold, unyielding floor beneath me. I was in hell and couldn't escape it.

But that was only my perception, however the reality was different. I was in an induced coma, a ventilator breathing for me, my body fighting for survival. One lung had collapsed, and COVID was attacking my body. The medical team was doing everything they could to keep me alive. And the reason I felt like I was face down? Because I was. Before COVID reached the UK, medical teams had studied cases from China and discovered that proning: placing patients on their stomachs, improved survival rates. So, every 48 hours, the team carefully turned me, repositioning my body to give my lungs the best chance of functioning.

Two weeks passed. Then, they attempted to take me off the ventilator. What follows is my account, my version of what I believed was happening: My eyelids slowly opened, heavy like lead. Blinking through the haze, I slowly took in my surroundings. A nun stood directly in front of me. I shifted my gaze to the left. More nuns. Four of them, all staring, no, boring their eyes into mine with an intensity that felt almost intimidating. Where am I? I strained to listen. Spanish accents. A convent? In Spain? Panic surged through me as I tried to move, but my arms and legs remained unresponsive. Still paralyzed. Yet, for the first time, I could see. Not only that, but the nuns also seemed to be communicating with me...had I regained the ability to speak?! Before I could attempt a word, a sudden commotion erupted outside.

I watched as the nuns and what looked like security officers rushed to the doors, hurriedly barricading them shut. BANG! A deafening crash rattled the windows. The nuns stiffened; their faces etched with panic. BANG! Louder this time. The sound echoed through the room, piercing my ears, and then I heard it. "We are under attack by the IRA!"

Terror gripped me. I needed to escape, to save myself, but how? My body refused to move. A shadow loomed over me. A nun approached, her face eerily calm. I barely registered the large syringe clutched behind her back until she was right beside me. Pressing a finger to her lips, she whispered, "Shhh… hush now. You need to pass over. It's time to die." No.

I tried to scream, to protest, but my voice failed me. My children, they needed me! I couldn't die. Not now. Not like this. Yet the cold, cruel realization hit me like a thunderclap, she was about to euthanize me. This was it. My death, thrust upon me, whether I liked it or not. Candles flickered as the nuns gathered, solemnly overseeing my final moments. The liquid flowed in and my eyelids drooped, the world slipping away. Then—suddenly—my eyes snapped back open. Aha! Look at me! I'm defying medicine. YOU WON'T KILL ME! But then—darkness.

Of course, as you're reading this, you already know I didn't die. Instead, I was experiencing delirium. In reality, the nurses had realised that my body wasn't ready. After attempting to remove me from the ventilator, my condition worsened, and they had to re-intubate me. The injection I thought was meant to kill me, in fact was sedation, preparing me to be placed back under. And so more days passed. The second time they removed the ventilator, my body finally responded. I had survived, and so my long road to recovery began.

Recovery And Awakening

COVID had ravaged my body, leaving me weak, but my warrior spirit refused to surrender. And so, the next stage began: recovery. As I was led out of ICU, emotion swelled in my chest. A guard of honour lined the corridor—doctors, nurses, the very heroes who had saved my life and here they were, clapping, cheering, celebrating me. Tears blurred my vision, I let the moment wash over me, engraving their faces into my soul. I had survived. However, survival was merely the beginning. I was taken to the rehabilitation ward, where I faced my next battle: learning to walk again.

Each trembling step was one step closer to home and to my boys and my partner, whom I hadn't seen in weeks due to the relentless grip of the pandemic. Whilst my body fought to heal, I noticed something profound...everything around me seemed sharper. Brighter. More alive. I was seeing the world in colour—as if I had been asleep all my life and only now had truly woken up. Not just to life but to purpose! A deep, unshakable knowing ignited within me. This wasn't just survival; this was now my time to thrive.

On the day of my discharge, the hospital staff informed me they were keeping a record of COVID survivors, patients who had made it through and were finally being reunited with their families, nonetheless sadly so many hadn't made it. My statistic/my number was 111. Something inside me stirred. A powerful, electric sensation surged through my soul. I knew this number meant something. As soon as I looked it up, the realization hit me like a bolt of lightning: 111. A divine number. A portal to spiritual awakening. A sign from the universe that I was being called to something greater. At that moment, I understood. My survival wasn't just chance. It was destiny.

Finding My Purpose

Upon discharge, I was handed a badge embossed with the words "Rehab Legend" by the incredible rehab sister, Kate Tantum. At the time, I didn't fully grasp the meaning behind it. But now, five years

The Journey

on, it holds immense significance. So much has changed. My spiritual growth has been profound, and the path I walk today is a world away from the one I was living before COVID. I have forged a new way forward, one now filled with divine enlightenment. Yet alongside that growth runs the lingering impact of critical illness. The toll COVID took on my body still affects my daily life, and my rehabilitation remains ongoing, perhaps it always will?

But in my search for healing, I discovered something profound: energy work. Experiencing firsthand the transformative power of holistic healing, I felt called to learn it for myself, starting with Reiki (shout out here to my amazing friend and trainer, Anne) and as I began delving deeper into healing, a whole new world unfolded before me. Joining the VIP Manifesting Academy and working under the guidance of Gemma Williams allowed me to truly envision and manifest a life I had always longed for. Although as I continued exploring different healing modalities, I felt something was still missing.

I was being pulled toward something higher. That's when I discovered The Starlight Temple and one of the most gifted channellers, Kahreela. Through her teachings, I embarked on a five-month channelling course that has completely transformed my abilities. Now, I can call upon spiritual guides, channel messages, and offer guidance, not just for myself, but for others, and that has become my true passion—guiding others spiritually while facilitating their healing.

This chapter is only a glimpse of my journey. The delirium alone could fill three chapters, and so there is still so much more to share. I intend to release my full story, as I know it holds lessons, inspiration, and hope for others walking their own paths. During the writing of this book collaboration, I was forced to relive ICU in an entirely new way—this time, through my mother's critical illness. Facing those memories again was painful, but my spiritual connection and the unwavering support of those around me helped me stay strong.

If there's one thing, I want you to take from my story, it's this: We are all so much stronger than we think. Even in our darkest moments, we have the power to overcome the impossible!

If you'd like to connect with me, you can find me here:

Full name: **Sadie Hallett-Chambers**

Email: **sadiethestar@gmail.com**

Facebook: **https://www.facebook.com/share/1CRrwHqCd5/?mibextid=wwXIfr**

Instagram: **https://www.instagram.com/sadie_hc_111?igsh=ZGF1MGo5YXh2NnJ1&utm_source=qr**

TikTok: **https://www.tiktok.com/@sadiethestar?_t=ZN-8uIfiVsk9p8&_r=1**

Chapter Six

By Alicia Harris

Alone

From the day I came into this world, I have felt alone.... rejected from the time I was in my mother's womb. I was unwanted by her and denied by my birth father and his family. Although many think it is impossible to know or feel like such, I disagree as I feel and have experienced how this affects us in many ways throughout our lives. We feel rejected, we feel when we are not loved, we feel when we are seen as a burden, we feel when we are not wanted, we feel when we are hated, and we definitely feel when the person who birthed us blames us for their problems.

Being born into a strict Catholic Irish family out of wedlock, shame already hung over me before I was even born, as well as my mother and grandmother who was pregnant at more or less the same time as her daughter which caused more upset and shame. I can only imagine how my mother felt and what was said to her during the pregnancy, especially as my birth father rejected her and left for England so as not to be held accountable or responsible for his choices and actions.

I do feel empathy for her, but it does not excuse her choices or how she treated me throughout my life. This was my childhood... feeling unloved, like a burden, hated and unwanted. I believe when we feel these emotions and feelings from such a young age it creates unworthiness within, we lack self-love, self-care and become "people pleasers" in a way of trying to please for attention or to please just to feel that little inkling of attention or love. This has followed me throughout my life.

I am now 46 years old, a sole parent to 5 children and still in many ways feel alone, not as much as I used to as I have worked a lot on myself and on finding me. Sometimes this feeling is connected within as I/we don't understand fully why things happened as they did and when I/we actually learn it's not our fault it is hard to accept as I/we have always been told that it's me that's the problem, issue, wrong etc. And unfortunately, I grew up believing so. On this journey we call life I have experienced so many lessons as we all do including some very hard ones, but as I grow, connect within, and continue finding "me" I am discovering my authentic self, hoping that one day I will no longer feel alone.

Child Sexual Abuse

I feel this is such a hard topic for many and often swept under the carpet and ignored. But unfortunately, it's very real. All around this world and a reality for many, more than we think. I experienced child sexual abuse from the age of 4 until the age of about 13 by my grandfather and stepfather. I remember telling my aunt about this but was ignored and told to say rosary and ask for forgiveness. When I was still in the womb, my mother and her mother wanted to give me to the nuns, but her father refused this and stated no blood of his would be adopted as long as he lived. When I look at the one baby photo I have seen of me being held by my mother with my aunt and her husband all I see is sadness, emptiness, anger and resentment. This again is felt as a rejection, not being wanted and not loved. It is awful to see such in one's baby photo.

My bed was a drawer and although no one talks about my birth, or me as a child as it was all such a big secret, I was such a big shame on the family and known as the bastard child. I can imagine it was difficult for my "mother" too as she would have been called all kinds of names and was known as having a bastard child, but she had plenty of support from her family especially her older sisters and father. As I am now a mother of 5 children, I just cannot understand how this didn't make her want to love and protect me. Instead, I feel she just rejected and hated me more and more. My mother was my grandfather's pet, according to my aunts, but when I came along, he doted on me and we had a close bond.

This too caused a lot of upset as my grandmother was pregnant and felt resentment and jealousy which to a certain extent is understandable. But I also question as a woman and a mother where her compassion was. Where was her love and support for her daughter who became a young mother? I won't go into too much of my experience of child sexual abuse as that's a book in itself, but I do want to touch on it a bit to bring awareness to it and most importantly for others who experienced child sexual abuse to know your truth is valid and you are not alone.

As a young girl my grandfather was in my eyes the most amazing person in the world, and I idolized him. He took me everywhere, always hugging and kissing me and he was the only person who showed me any love and affection. Little did I know at the time that he was grooming me. He was always telling me not to tell that I'd had 7up, a bar, outings to shops, bookies etc. Always being treated with ice cream, sweets, crisps and treats but never to tell.

This made me feel special, loved and cared for but I never saw the dark side of it and that's the innocence of a child. This led to a kiss on the lips, a longer kiss when he would say "show me how much you love me" and then the touching started. Always sitting on his lap, he would kiss my neck and tell me to kiss his etc. etc. I was only 3 when it started, and I didn't know it was wrong as after all he was the only person that loved me in my little mind. My mother was dating and eventually got married. I lived most of my life with my grandparents as far as I can remember, and my mom had 3 more children with her husband. At first, he was told that I was her little sister (more lies and shame) then he agreed to adopt me, against his father's and family's wishes. Again, I was shamed and frowned upon.

My stepfather was a very angry man and drank a lot. My childhood memories of them as a couple are not great, they drank, they argued, and he had affairs. I still spent most of my time at my grandparents but my first memory of child sexual abuse by him was when my mother went to Blackpool on a girl's weekend. I was about 7. I remember him drinking with others and when they left, he came into my room. His smell was sickening. He was muttering and touching me breathing heavily and kept saying "you're not mine, its ok you're not mine". I was sobbing and I am sure I left my body as it was just awful. This continued until I was about 13/14. I am sure my family knew especially my mother, but no one ever helped me and anytime I said anything I was told I was a liar, evil, demonic etc. Through the years child sexual abuse had a huge effect on me, how I saw myself and relationships both with friends and boyfriends as I never trusted anyone and always felt I wasn't good enough in every level of life. I was used, manipulated, laughed at, ignored and shamed most of my life. All I wanted was to be liked and loved for who I am. This I believe is why as an adult I attracted a narcissist.

Who Am I? The Big Question

At the age of 18 on my birthday my stepfather told me about my birth father after years of asking. None of my family would tell me about him, especially not my mother. She had herself convinced that I thought my stepfather was my actual father. This always showed me that she lived her life in lies and was completely disconnected from the truth. Everyone's answer when I asked about my birth father was, "Don't be opening cans of worms, don't upset your mother." This always infuriated me as no one ever thought about my feelings, hurt and pain. This is not in any form of self-pity but an acknowledgment of how people can disregard a child/ person and make one feel more unworthy.

We had moved to Holland when I was almost 11 and life was not great over there. My parents drank more, partied more, and starting school and learning a new language was hard. I got depressed, developed an eating disorder and tried to commit suicide as I just couldn't cope with the sexual, physical and mental abuse, lies and neglect anymore. My mother hated me and showed it in every possible way, and everything got worse when we moved there. At age 18 I came back to Ireland on holiday, and I started looking for my birthfather. All I had was his name and the area his mother lived in. I knocked on lots of doors asking if they knew him but with no luck. I got more depressed and sadder as no one cared or wanted to help.

For 3 years I looked for him, and begged family to tell me more but no one wanted to upset my "mother". Just before my 21st birthday we had a family wedding in Ireland and my Godmother pressed my mom to tell me as I was asking her, and she felt bad. That weekend I was to babysit my cousins, but my aunt insisted I go out with them. I really didn't want to, but she insisted. When I arrived at the pub my "mother" was nowhere to be seen, my uncle was acting a bit odd and said, "your mom is over there." As I walked over, I got a weird sensation in my tummy and when I got to the table there was a man sitting with my mother and I said, "is this him?" I just knew he was my birthfather. I actually look more like him than I do my mother's family.

That night he told me he had 5 children, and he'd brought his eldest daughter in to meet me. I was so overwhelmed and confused, she knew all along where he was and never told me. Knowing I was looking for him for the last 3 years. He asked if I'd like to see his other kids, I wasn't sure, but my "mother" insisted and stated she was a part of this, and I was not to exclude her. Again, it was all about her. I felt sick. How could he have 5 children and never think of getting in touch with me? Why ask if I wanted to meet his wife and other children when I had only just met him?

Everything was going so fast my head was spinning and I'd never seen my "mother" behave as she was now. Who was this person? After some time of getting to know him, he asked if I would come stay with them to be a part of his family and asked me to take his surname. I thought I was wanted and maybe the grass was greener. I was wrong. After moving in with them I realized his wife suffered severe mental health, he was an alcoholic and compulsive gambler, it all became chaotic, toxic and again abuse had followed me here too. This seems to be a pattern in my life. Who am I?

Domestic Violence

After all the chaos and toxicity, I threw myself into work. I worked in Customer Service and did beauty and nails working long hours and went out with friends after work to distract my mind from all my shitty experiences. I went to my friend's cousin's wedding as her plus 1 and met my now ex there. It started off great but then he became controlling, overprotective, paranoid and 100 percent narcissistic. I stayed in the controlling and physically and mentally abusive relationship as he got right in my head and because of all my experiences I felt I didn't deserve any better. We had 4 children and when my eldest son was 9, he saved my life. That's when I knew it was time to leave, I am lucky and very blessed to be alive and I know if I didn't leave then I'd not be sitting here today.

I was contacted by Carol from 'Sisters Of Charity' as the school had contacted them with concerns. She had knocked on the door and my then broken self opened the door slightly and said, "please help me." Carol helped me pack a black bag and took my then 4 children and I to a woman's refuge. This too wasn't a great experience but a great lesson.

These places are too very controlling and not a nice environment, but I met a lovely lady who came weekly to do some holistic treatments and she introduced me to Reiki & meditation, which helped get me through each day. From the woman's refuge we became homeless and spent 3 years moving between various homeless accommodations. Then with the help, love and support from the most beautiful Earth Angel Carol we finally got our forever home.

I am now a sole parent of 5 beautiful children and have been parenting them completely by myself for the last 10 years. Their "dad" chooses not to see them or to pay maintenance for them. I do not engage with any of my family including my "mother" as I choose me, the truth and my children. I would never have gotten through those 3 years without Carol, she cried with me, hugged me and held my hand through the hardest, loneliest and most degrading part of my life. Carol was my rock, my support and my blessing. She was the mother I never had but always wished for. I am forever grateful for her all her love, support and guidance and Carol will always hold a big place in my heart.

My Healing Journey

After we got the keys to our forever home, life was just crazy as a sole parent of 5 young children, there was never a dull day. At this time in my life, I started to feel very guilty, blaming myself for everything that had happened and to go deep within myself. Then one day Reiki kept popping up everywhere. I started going to a beautiful soul Jennifer for healings, I joined her Moon Mná group and started my Reiki journey with her. In no time I was a Reiki master, and from there I did a beautiful Sister Circle course and became a Sister Circle Leader. I was not yet ready to facilitate others, but I was healing myself and filling my bag with tools to eventually facilitate others to open up to self-healing as it's within us all.

I joined an online group, The VIP Manifesting Academy and learned about self-love, self-care, manifesting and lots of healing modalities and courses. I knew this was my journey and that all I had experienced was for a reason. I went on to meet lots of beautiful people who were teaching holistic therapies. Amazing Abi taught me Rihanni healing, beautiful Sharon crystal therapy, psychic development & card reading energy healing and so much more. The more I learned the more I was healing deep within and the more I knew I could help others.

I recently started having hypnosis with Sharon and this too is absolutely amazing. It confirmed my truths, wiped away lots of my self-doubt and fears, and helped me to truly connect to my true authentic self on a deeper level. I had many bad days and lots of good days, there were days I couldn't get out of bed, and I learned it's ok to listen to your body and to just be.

We live, we learn, we grow, and we heal. I have learned not to be too hard on myself, that no one is perfect and what others think of me is not my business. I still have my good and bad days, self-doubt and fears, it's part of life but I can deal with it all much better. Now I truly know my journey is to facilitate others on their healing journey with love, compassion, and non-judgment. We are all as one on this journey we call life, let's stand in love and unite.

Believing In Me

So, after all my experiences in this life so far, I am finally at a place of contentment and able to believe in me. I still have some obstacles to overcome, and I will continue to learn to help heal myself and add to my tools to facilitate others on their healing journeys. I can now confidently speak my truths without any voices of others in my head denying me. I now accept my beautiful kind and caring heart fully and now know my softness is a pure gift.

The Journey

I see Mother Mary as my real and only Mother and know she helped me through my difficult times with love and compassion. I have forgiven all who hurt, abused me and tried to destroy me and this forgiveness is for me, and I know they have their own demons to face, and I believe in Karma. I believe in me, and I hope whoever is reading this, that you believe in you too. Our uniqueness is truly our superpower and our greatest gift. I believe in me, and I believe in you. You are amazing, worthy, needed and loved. Remember beautiful hearts, you are loved, you are love and everything you seek is within you. See, feel and believe it is so.

Always believe in yourself and shine bright beautiful soul xx

If you wish to, you can follow me on Facebook & Instagram **@Heavenly Stars Healing**

Chapter Seven

By Lynsey Cowie

Introduction

I'm Lynsey, I'm a Reiki Master and a Silver Violet Flame Master. I'm qualified in various other energy healing modalities, and I also work with plant medicines. I've been through and dealt with a lot of trauma including domestic abuse, drug addiction, eating disorders, anxiety, depression and CPTSD. I've experienced 2 suicides of people very close to me, lost many friends to suicide and addiction and I am undiagnosed ADHD.

There isn't much I can't empathise with. I now realise I went through everything that I have to find a way of healing myself and others. It's my soul purpose to support other women to face their trauma, heal and to empower themselves. I love what I do, and I know I'm good at it.

I grew up in Aberdeen Scotland. I came from what would be considered a good home with really loving parents. My dad was a Chief Inspector in the Police- he was a mental health nurse before joining the police and again when he retired after 30 years' service. My Mum was a nurse, midwife, health visitor, AIDS councillor, and had a degree in psychology- she had her own practice as a private councillor.

I grew up in a beautiful home with my parents and my older brother, I never wanted for anything, in a material sense. My dad was a kind, patient, beautiful soul, a real 'hands on' Dad. He regularly took me fishing, swimming and out hunting for ferrets with the family dog. He taught me to ride a bike, and we spent a lot of time in nature, going for walks and tending to his garden. My dad was my absolute hero!!

My Mum was an elegant woman who liked the finer things in life. She was a very strong woman, a woman who demanded respect. We had a very difficult relationship at times, it wasn't easy living up to her expectations and that brought us many struggles, but she taught me so much about myself. She was quite extravagant and loved the finer things in life whilst my dad was very humble and wasn't about money, he had tight family values. They clearly loved each other; they were married for 43 years!

Despite my family being loving, I felt like I was different or like something was missing or I was looking for something, I couldn't put my finger on it. As a young child, I remember being so in tune with other people and could always sense when something was wrong or not right. I was hypersensitive and didn't know at this point that I was in tune with energy. I didn't see it as a gift until a few years ago. It was a curse as far as I was concerned, I didn't want to feel all the shitty feelings I felt because I didn't understand them. My dad called me a free spirit, my mum called me "the wild child" which I think was a nice way of saying I was a nightmare!

The Nightmare Begins

At 12 years old I was groomed and sexually abused. It continued for over a year. I thought it was my fault, I felt so dirty and ashamed. I never told anyone, I didn't want anyone thinking of me what I thought of myself, and I couldn't face breaking my dads heart. I also assumed my dad would report it as he was in the police, and I couldn't face the shame. The shame I thought I'd bring upon my family, so I kept it quiet, and I found drink and drugs which helped to keep my feelings suppressed, or so I thought. By the time I was 18 I ended up in rehab. My family so desperately wanted me to get clean and I wanted to get clean to please my family and gain their approval. But deep down I liked how drugs made me not feel the things I didn't want to feel. I could see the hurt I was causing everyone around me, but I couldn't comprehend it. I felt disconnected from it- I guess the drugs helped. I remember my mum telling me that I had been anaesthetising myself for years but that my family didn't have the luxury of that, and they had to face the pain. I now know that my lack of self-love made it difficult for me to understand how loved I was by my family.

I got into a long-term relationship with a guy called Craig who was a well-known criminal that would last off and on for 19 years of my life. My family knew it was an unhealthy relationship, but I always tried to hide the severity of the situation. I can recall him breaking my nose and my dad asking me how I'd got 2 black eyes. I lied, some bullshit excuse about falling ice skating. I could tell by the look on his face that he knew I was lying but when you're lost in that, you lie because the truth is so shameful and too painful to face.

My Dads Suicide

About a month before my dad passed away, he'd come up to Craigs mums house for fireworks. I was a bit boozy and told him I loved him, not knowing that was the last time I'd see him alive. He told me he loved me too but just didn't love some of the things I did. I knew he was referring to my drug addiction and being with my choice of partner.

On the 10th of December 2010, I got the most devastating call of my life, it was my Mum, "your dads dead, he hung himself because of you." It didn't make sense, my dad was so against suicide, he'd always comment how "it was the cowards way out" and that it left devastation behind. He'd seen it in his job first hand so I know this will may sound weird, but I always thought he'd never leave the world that way. He was fit and healthy, so I never even thought about him dying let alone by his own hands.

The Journey

I now understand my Mum was angry and it was easy to blame me, I blamed me! I'd caused so much hurt and pain through my addictions and questionable life choices, but no one blamed me more than I did myself. It felt like it was my fault and my fault alone that my dad had committed suicide. That was the day the rug was pulled from under my feet and my whole world fell apart- I'd only just been keeping it together too but my dad, my hero, my rock, my stability was gone.

My Mum and I had a difficult relationship, and my dad was the peacekeeper, with him gone and the thought of him leaving this world alone and feeling he had no other choice but to take his own life absolutely devastated me. The guilt of everything I'd ever done or not done absolutely consumed me and I spiralled so out of control that the 6 years after my dad's passing is a bit of a blur. I just remember I could never face the month of December or Christmas- he was cremated on Christmas Eve and I wasn't welcome at his funeral. I sat outside in my car and watched everyone going in as a Piper piped "Amazing Grace." I hit self-destruct and my addiction to heroin, crack cocaine and various prescription tablets spiralled. In June 2016 I accidentally overdosed and ended up in a coma. Ironically, that's what saved my life.

When my dad died, Craig was in prison. I was so hurt and angry he wasn't there when I needed him the most. This was the beginning of the end of this relationship, but it would take me another 10 years to break free. I had a trauma bond with Craig, it was like an addiction, I loved him, but I also hated him- he'd been my protector but also my abuser. I tried to move on with my life. I reconnected with a man I'd loved since I was 16, Sime (Simon). He was a truly decent man. I knew I could trust him and rely on him. I felt safe with him. Life was improving but my addiction, guilt, shame and pain were still there. I'd become so good at masking my emotional pain, but it was now making me physically ill- I had been diagnosed with fibromyalgia a couple of years after my dad died.

The Coma

The day I overdosed it was a miracle I was found in time. My neighbours hadn't seen my car move nor the steam from my heating coming out of the pipe in the wall, so we reckon I'd been lying there for 16 hours. They called an ambulance. On arrival to A&E, my body core temperature was 23 degrees, I had pulmonary pneumonia in both my lungs, septicaemia- my body had necrosis, I was effectively starting to decompose.

My Mum was advised to switch off my life support as if I made it through the night I'd have suffered from hypoxia (starvation of oxygen to the brain) and be left in a vegetive state for the rest of my life. But Sime refused to give up on me and wouldn't let the life support be turned off. I woke up a week later. I knew that my dad had been watching over me. While apparently brain dead, my soul was floating about the universe doing its own thing. It was so vivid, so real and that was my proof that there is something beyond this physical existence we call life.

On awakening from the coma, I was told it was a miracle I'd survived and that I wouldn't walk again with the damage done to my leg while lying on the kitchen floor for so long. My focus at that point was to prove everyone wrong and to walk again. There was no way I was never walking again!! Sime was so supportive and did so much to help me physically and emotionally. I wouldn't be here if it wasn't for him. He really truly loved me, but the problem was I didn't love myself. We had a lot of other things going on in our lives at the time, life was really stressful especially for Sime. 11 months later, Sime and I split up and a few days later he also committed suicide.

Rock Bottom

I was on heavy painkillers, including fentanyl, since the coma but it didn't soften the blow of Simes suicide. I again went into self blame and felt heavy guilt. I hadn't even processed the guilt of my dad's suicide yet. Within a year of that, my Mum died of cancer and even though we didn't always see eye to eye, her death and the fact we weren't on speaking terms broke me even more than I ever thought possible. I felt truly alone.

I spent about 6 months on my sofa, sobbing, barely eating, only sleeping when I was exhausted enough, taking painkillers to help me switch off from the mental and physical pain I was in. On top of the fibromyalgia, I now had severe nerve pain and sciatica, the physical pain was absolute torture. I tried to take my own life, what I took should have killed me 3 times over but it didn't- I couldn't even get that shit right! I then felt nothing but guilt that I'd been selfish enough to want my pain to stop so badly that I was prepared to leave my 2 boys feeling like my dad had left me feeling and I hated myself for that.

The thing is, when you're in that much pain, you truly believe that you're better off dead and that you're doing your loved ones a favour. It is selfish but it is also sheer desperation. I'm lucky that my attempt didn't work, it wasn't my time to go! Again, I had consultants telling me it was a miracle I was still alive and that I didn't need a liver transplant. I didn't feel like a miracle, I felt like one big, massive failure as a woman, as a mother, as a daughter and as a partner.

Taking My Power Back

I tried to leave Craig for many years. I took him back so many times over the years but the last time I was with him, I really resented him, and myself for letting him back into my life to cause more destruction. He wasn't easy to say no to and often I took him back, but I knew it wasn't going to work.

He turned nasty again and broke my rib. This wasn't the first time he'd laid hands on me, he'd stabbed me before, but this time was different. I had no pity for him or fear of him. I felt hatred towards him. I knew if he didn't kill me, I would kill him in self defence so after some persuasion from the police, I gave a statement. I vowed that I'd make my dad, Sime and my mum proud. It had taken their deaths for me to realise I had to sort my life out and be someone that they, my boys and I could be proud of. I couldn't let myself lose anyone else over him.

5 years ago I testified in court against him. It was one of the hardest things I've ever had to do but I knew it was do or die at this point. I did a midnight flit 4 and a half years ago when he was due out of prison for domestic abuse. He was given a 3 year non harassment order, so I now had 3 years to breathe.

Time To Do Me!

Although my "spiritual awakening" started from when I was in a coma in 2016, I still had a lot of hard work to do. Here I was in a new house in a strange town, heavily addicted to painkillers, housebound, none of my remaining family speaking to me. My parents and the partner who showed me nothing but love and support, all gone. My physical health was poor, my mobility wasn't great, and I was in so much physical and emotional pain that I couldn't even get out of bed most days.

I then found a mentor who taught me about emotional alchemy- facing your emotions and letting yourself feel what you're feeling but then once you've leaned into the emotion, drop the story you keep telling yourself that's keeping you stuck in that emotion. As I changed my thinking from, "why is this happening TO me?" to "why is this happening FOR me?" I started to see the lesson to be taken from every bad situation in my life.

I had to learn to forgive myself and love myself which wasn't easy after the destruction I'd caused. I had to stop blaming myself and others for the way I'd ended up and take responsibility for my life. I also had to learn to nurture my inner child and to give her everything she'd needed and wanted her whole life. I had to learn to be kind to myself and not beat myself up anymore.

I came off the painkillers, I'd realised that the fentanyl, pregabalin, morphine and various other drugs weren't killing my pain, they were actually causing it and killing ME! They were causing my physical healing to slow down.

The more I faced my shit, the less I was in physical pain. It was also around this time I was introduced to Reiki and energy healing, and I was blown away by the power of it. This was doing way more for me than any doctor or surgeon had done. By the time I thought I'd made peace with everything in my mind, I stepped into the world of plant medicine as I was on a mission to heal myself without the "help" I'd been offered from the NHS.

I started using plant medicines- Chaga, cacao, then kambo and psilocybin, which helped me to deal with things on a soul/cellular level. The pieces were starting to come together, I was finally making peace with myself and my past.

When my exes non harassment order was up, I knew I had to close the book on that one myself, so I faced him. I'd seen him in town and knew I had to stand in my power. My legs were shaking, my heart beating out of my chest, but I still walked up to him. I hugged him and said I was sorry to hear about his dads passing. He tried his usual manipulation tactics, but I told him I would never go back with him but and that I wished him all the best. I also thanked him for the lessons he'd given me in life because I took them, and I made myself strong in spite of them. That's taking your power back, and it felt good.

The Journey

I mentioned before that I couldn't face the month of December or Christmas; I just wanted it to fuck off! 4 years ago, I decided to celebrate my dad's life and what he'd brought to mine instead of mourning his death. I'd spent 10 years being miserable at Christmas and over the last few years I made myself embrace it to the point where last Christmas I was actually excited for it. I'd done it, I'd turned that dark period of my life around.

I don't feel guilt or shame surrounding my past now, I'm proud of who I am today- I am loving, I am passionate about what I do, I am empathetic, I am strong, I am loved, and I am enough. I'm not just surviving anymore, I'm thriving. I'm aware of my emotions and how to navigate them properly now. I feel energy now and I trust what I'm feeling.

I became a member of Gemma's VIP Manifesting Academy 2 years ago because I wanted to learn reiki and energy work. I'd been looking for a teacher for a while and I can't even remember how I came across Gemma- all I know is there are no coincidences and I found her for a reason.

I've gotten more than just a reiki teacher from the VIP, I've got the most amazing mentor, friend and valuable connection in Gemma, a tribe of women who "get it" and we all support each other and cheer each other on.

I've been learning loads of different energy healing modalities and how to serve plant medicines and I've stepped out of my comfort zone and started to believe in myself and trust my intuition. It's not an easy process but it's such a rewarding one. If I can do it anyone can!!

https://www.facebook.com/profile.php?id=100075144642652&mibextid=wwXIfr

https://www.facebook.com/profile.php?id=61566558174339&mibextid=wwXIfr

@lynsey_1111 on Instagram

@lynsey.cowie on TikTok

Chapter Eight

By Sabrina Faulkner

Introduction

I never thought I would be sat in an office surrounded by paperwork and logos and a website, and it is all mine! Me, a single mom with a chronic illness, the owner of my own successful business in a field of work that I love and have wanted to do forever. If ever we wanted to talk about imposter syndrome now would be the time. I spent 8 years training to become a doctor in psychology, but it never worked out. It never quite got me where I felt I needed to be, so I had to go back to the drawing board and work my way through to becoming a Psychotherapist.

It felt at times like it was never going to happen but when it got to the point of working with client's the amount of satisfaction and joy it brought was unexplainable. It was a snowball effect from there, it went so quickly between seeing people on placements to actually working for myself. I was determined to make this business a success, and in this chapter, I will share how I went from feeling hopeless to being helpful. I want to share my learnings in the hopes of enabling others to know they too can strive for success and more importantly there is always help whenever you need it. Never stop aspiring for your goals.

Failure Again

Another failed business venture and here I was with tears stinging the back of my eyes as I loaded up my jeep with all my beauty room equipment. I just didn't understand how setting up a beauty room in the back of a hairdressers could possibly fail. I offered every up-to-date treatment, and I even offered low prices but still no one came. With the jeep loaded up I drove home, but I refused to cry and vowed to I find a way to make it work for me.

I had a spare room in my house, so the mission began to turn that into a possible beauty room and maybe try and keep my business going this way and not to lose heart. My daughter and I set the room up and it looked amazing. I advertised on social media to reach as many people as possible and now it was a waiting game.

A couple of weeks went by, and I got one customer, my neighbour who wanted her nails done and it felt good just to have someone anyone, but it wasn't enough. I had so many things in this room that were just sitting around and not being used and I started to feel like "what is the point?" The weeks went by, and I kept on advertising but nothing and the room was just sat empty. I finally made the decision that I had to stop what I was doing and sell the things in my room so they could be of use to someone else and make some of my money back.

I hadn't realised the impact that this had on me and once the room had been cleared of most things my days seemed a lot greyer, and my thoughts revolved around how I always seemed to fail at everything I did. I couldn't understand how I was unable to achieve anything I set my mind to. I had been to university and got a degree and made no use of it because it hadn't helped me get the job I wanted. I wanted to work in counselling or psychotherapy. I had tried to do something completely different, and I had failed again. The grey somehow turned to a very dark cloud and the days passed me by in this darkness.

Illness Strikes

I continued to do the everyday things such as being mom but in the process along the way I became unwell. Once I had shook this off the GP had asked to see me for a flu injection. As someone who has multiple sclerosis (MS), I was always advised against the injection, but the GP felt it would be advisable on this occasion given how low I had been feeling. I took the flu injection and thought nothing more of it until the following morning.

During the night my leg had started to tingle, and I didn't want to panic and think I was having an MS relapse, so I tried to stay calm. I rang NHS 111, they had never heard of MS so they could not advise me on what to do, so again I remained calm and hoped it would pass. By the early hours of the morning the tingling had reached up to my arm, and I was very scared. I did not want to frighten my daughter to I continued as normal and sent her off to school which was walking distance from the house and this time call 999. I explained the situation however they could not get an ambulance to me for another 4 hours. I had to make my own way to the hospital. I had to call a taxi.

The taxi driver was so kind he could see I was very unwell. He didn't charge me for the drive to the hospital and he even took me into the emergency department because at this point, I could no longer walk. I could feel my body slowly shutting down. I remember being sat on a chair in the emergency department for some time and then being asked to stand but then nothing. I woke up in a bed with my family around me and struggling to speak not knowing what had happened. When they left one of the nurses told me that the doctor would be around later, and they would let me know what had happened.

I had a MS relapse which triggered a mini stroke, and I needed to rest as they needed to find out the cause of the relapse. I got moved to a ward with senior females that were near end of life or who had suffered a stroke. The feeling of helplessness suddenly became so real because I could not move the one side of my body, and the fear of would I be able to again suddenly became frightening.

Moving On

It took me 16 weeks to get over the relapse in hospital however, the stroke had a bigger impact than expected. I had to learn to do my motor skills all over again. I had to learn to walk and write and feed myself. When I came home it also became apparent that my home needed certain adaptions to help me get around it that were not going to be approved by my landlord, so decisions needed to be made about my living situation.

I needed to find somewhere else to live. This was not an ideal time as covid was in full force and things were becoming much more difficult to arrange, but by the skin of my teeth I was able to get a new house with the help of family and move in just as the country was put into lockdown. Over the next coming weeks, the hospital team did come in and put in the necessary adaptions for me and my MS team where able to come to my house to give me treatment, so I was very lucky.

The one thing that was suggested to me by my MS nurse was speaking to a therapist. I hadn't spoken to a therapist in years and to be honest I hadn't stuck to any of my previous therapists because I just felt like they were very uptight. I said I would think about it as I often journalled and had done my whole life. I had always found this helpful so maybe speaking to someone could be of use too.

I always wanted to a therapist myself that is why I did psychology, but I found out afterwards that doing psychology isn't the right route. I kept thinking about speaking to a therapist and finding someone that might be more suitable for me so I went on the counselling directory to see if I could pick out three to contact and see how I get on from there.

Out of the three only two came back to me and one was more suited to men's therapy. The lady I picked looked very friendly and warm. I set up a meeting and she was brilliant. We had an instant bond. She helped me with my personal concerns, and she helped me find my way with my route to becoming a psychotherapist. She pointed me in the direction of what I needed to do and how I needed to do it, and it was as if someone had sent me a lifeline towards everything I ever wanted. I had weekly therapy sessions and every time I would come away feeling better and more confident about what I needed to do.

I Can Do This!

Lockdown came to an end, and I applied for my therapy course and training. I had to do an interview over zoom as the course director had broken her leg. She was so well spoken, and she just looked outstanding. I was honest about myself, and I could see her concern was that I was financially not her regular student, but I assured her that I would make every payment, and I would do my very best.

Walking into that classroom on the first day you could see the class difference straight away. It was clear I was from a middle to low class and everyone else was from a higher class, but I chose to come to the best counselling school. Over the time that I was at the counselling school I realised that I really was a salt of the earth person and the years I spent being ashamed of where I am from, I shouldn't have because things like my accent is what made me unique and likeable and actually an approachable person. I found that in my counselling training clients where more likely to come to me before some of the others because I am a naturally smiley person, and I looked like I was enjoying what I was doing.

The training was difficult in the sense that it made me really look at myself under a microscope and broaden my perspective on the world in general, and even though I felt I may be an open book how open was I really? It gave me a new profound understanding into so many areas and whilst it was difficult and challenging, I enjoyed every minute of it because I knew that this had always been my passion. This is what I had always wanted to do. To be able to work with people and know that whatever their situation is that you can help them in a way that is completely different to anyone else. It also gave me the goal to make help available to whoever needs it. My training taught me that so many people needed the help and were not able to access it due to funding or location or whatever the reason maybe.

SRF Therapy Services

I handed in my final assignment; I took the picture of my folder handed in and present and then I breathed a sigh of relief. All my hard work for 2 years was in that folder, all the assignments, all my client work, all my weekly journal reports on my journey to get there, and more importantly all my proof of all the therapy work I had done on myself with my counsellor to ensure I was ready to do this was there. I had put my all into this and it felt like my last chance at achieving what my heart had always desired.

I only allowed myself a short break from therapy work before I started to set up my own practice. I wanted to be ready so as soon as I got the green light to say I was qualified I was ready to go and start getting client work. I didn't want to sit and wait until later in the year or take a break. I wanted to get straight into helping people and getting my brand name out there. I believed I could do it. I believed I could make my business a success because I had the skills and ability.

The end of August came, and I got the email to say that I had qualified. I knew what I had to do; this was what I was always meant to do. The following morning, I got in touch with the ethical body, and I had my profile available and online for clients to be able to contact me for therapy. I also started contacting people I had worked with or knew in the therapy network to let them know I was now qualified and ready to take clients.

I qualified in August and by the October my client list was up to 25 clients plus a waiting list. I had never felt so humble and proud all at the same time. I had a wonderful support network in the form of my supervisor and my own therapist who I was still seeing on a regular basis and was able to get advice and guidance when I felt unsure. I was going from strength to strength.

Never Break A Promise

My therapy business continued to thrive, and I continued to enjoy every minute. I had agencies call me and ask if I would take clients or if I would work with them which was fantastic because my name was being passed around via networking. My client turn around was wonderful and they would leave me amazing feedback. I was getting awarded achievements from different online sites which was helping my business so much, but there was one thing in my mind that was staying with me that I hadn't quite achieved yet, and that was my personal goal to make help available to those who might need it the most.

I grew up in a low-income family and I knew what it was like to not have that person available to talk to when you needed it. The therapists I had were not the best and so I knew that in certain communities and locations they would not speak up and I had to find a way to combat this. I was a people person, and I wanted to give something back.

There is one thing that brings people together regardless of class and that thing is FOOTBALL! I replied to an advert on social media to be a sponsor for a local football club and in return they would wear my company logo on their shirts to raise awareness about therapy and it worked! I had people speaking to me at the side of pitches, before and after matches and everyone saw me as one of them and not as a therapist, and the boundaries started coming down. The boys from the team would wear the shirts to the gym or whilst out shopping and more and more people wanted to know about my company.

Word spread of what I was doing in the local communities and before I knew it, I had become a sponsor for a local boxer and for another football team. It also started to change the stigma around men's mental health as this was something that was not spoken about before, but now it was something that was spoken about more often and there was a point of contact that was completely confidential. I started attending football meetings and people higher up in the football leagues started to know my face and remember me.

A breezy Sunday morning with a coffee in my hand on the side of the pitch and everybody knows your name and they know your business and you know that you kept your promise, and you gave back what you could, and you are still finding ways to give back because I know that everybody needs somebody, there is no better feeling.

Get In Touch

If you are a newly qualified therapist and would like some advice and guidance on how to get started in private practice, I would be happy to offer you that support. I feel that the therapist community is one of the best when it comes to supporting each other and guiding each other. You can book a meeting with myself via my website.

Likewise, if you are someone who has read this and feels you need some support or just someone to speak to, I offer a free 30 minute chat on my website that you can book on to and we can have a talk and find out a way to give you some additional help with your concerns.

THE JOURNEY

Website: **www.srftherapyservices.co.uk**

Email: **srftherapyservices@gmail.com**

Instagram: **https://www.instagram.com/srf_therapy_services/**

Facebook: **https://www.facebook.com/profile.php?id=100091535052310**

Thank you

Chapter Nine

By Sharon Bedford

Addict To Healer

In this chapter, I share some of the darkest times in my life. Moments I was so broken I contemplated ending my life. I will openly share my struggles with addiction and the choices that cost me everything. I will also reveal how these struggles, filled with heartache, pain, and tragedy led me to moments of clarity and strength.

Pain is often something we fear and try to avoid. Yet through my journey, I learned that it is in our deepest pain, that we find our greatest strength. Pain is not something we endure and survive; it is the very force that pushes us to confront our shadows. Life is not about avoiding challenges but rising above them and evolving. Every obstacle is an opportunity to emerge stronger and become the person we were destined to be. Pain is not the end; it's the beginning of transformation. The universe doesn't speak in words, but in the stillness of our hearts.

Surviving In Silence

At 13/ 14, I was eager to fit in at my new high school after being bullied at my previous one. I was naïve, with no understanding of drugs. Naturally, I wanted to make friends and be accepted. My very first experience with heroin was with my friend and her boyfriend. I was casually handed some foil and told to inhale through a tube. From that moment, a wave of warmth engulfed me and it felt like being wrapped in cotton wool. Had I known what I know now, I can't say for certain if I would have turned it down. That pivotal moment became the beginning of two decades of addiction. Previously I had felt empty. Heroin for the first time, gave me a brief respite from pain, offering me a sense of comfort I had desperately craved in my turbulent teenage years.

One winter night, my friend and I were approached by a group of men. I think she was drawn to the attention; I wasn't interested at all. I hadn't even kissed a boy properly yet, so they didn't hold any appeal for me. My friend, on the other hand, was intrigued and left with one of them, leaving me alone with two strangers. I felt fear rising in my chest as one of the men grabbed my hand leading me around a corner.

My memories are blurry, as I've suppressed and buried the experience deep in my mind. I still recall the weight of his body on top of mine, the image of the innocent blue and white pants I wore haunt my mind's eye. I felt suffocated and completely unable to move. After what felt like an eternity, my friend appeared around the corner, this startled the man, and he got off.

My friend and I made our way to the bus stop, but the man followed us. I'll never understand why she did this, but she felt compelled to inform him that my parents were out for the evening. I was terrified, shaking uncontrollably the entire bus ride home, desperately trying to make eye contact with her to express my absolute fear, she didn't notice, did she even care? All these years later, I never understood why she did that to me, knowing the shy, timid girl I was.

I got off the bus and he followed me. I kept telling him that my parents would be home any minute. This had no impact on him whatsoever, he forced his way into my house and raped me again. However, this time was completely different, a level of fear I never thought possible shot through my body. The moment he finished, I immediately recoiled and distanced myself from him. I recall cradling and rocking myself backward and forward to comfort myself. He told me I was bleeding on the sofa, I hadn't even noticed, I just wanted him out of my house. I rushed upstairs to clean myself and came back downstairs. To my horror he was still there, he made a sarcastic comment about me not being a virgin anymore and left.

It has taken me many years to come to terms with the fact I didn't scream from the top of my lungs. I questioned myself over and over, WHY did I not seek help? I doubted myself, most of my life about this harrowing ordeal. I now understand this to be a completely normal reaction to a highly stressful situation, known as freeze and fawn. I was in a state of paralysis and could not move, nor could I shout for help.

I was scared to tell my parents, let alone the police, so I kept everything to myself. It wasn't until my early 20s, after having drinks with my family one evening, that I finally shared what happened, instinctively my parents phoned the police. However, the thought of involving the police felt overwhelming, and I ultimately decided not to take it any further.

The impact of that night haunted my teenage years, leaving me with no true understanding of what a healthy relationship looked like. Instead, all I knew was the experience of being taken advantage of. This warped my perception of what men expected from women. I found myself giving them whatever they wanted, thinking that was how things should be.

A Mother's Strength, A Woman's Pain

I experimented with heroin sporadically throughout my teens. At 16 it became easier to get hold of, and soon it developed into a weekly habit. When I was 17, I met Sean, we fell head over heels in love and moved in together not long after meeting. Heroin quickly became ingrained in our lives. Sean was into the usual party scene drugs, but never heroin. In a way, I feel responsible for his addiction and his death, as he began using alongside me. Our addiction escalated quickly, from weekend use to midweek use.

After several months of living together, Sean was sentenced to three years in prison for selling ecstasy to undercover police officers. Just days before his sentencing, I discovered I was pregnant, immediately stopped using drugs, and moved back in with my parents. I had no intention of returning to work, my full-time job would be raising my son.

From the very moment he was born he was my entire world. I had lots of support from my parents and Sean's mom. The first time Sean met his son was far from ideal, given that he was in prison, life was tough, but I coped the best I could.

Love Returned, But The Scars Remain

When our son was 10 months old, Sean came home, however, things began to escalate and drug use crept back in. At the time we lived in rented accommodation, but could no longer afford the rent, so we all moved in with Sean's mom. After a heated argument, my little boy and I were left homeless. Sean threw all our possessions onto the street. This was a new low, even for him. I felt so isolated and alone, with no one to turn to. My relationship with my parents had broken down, and I had no friends to lean on.

At first, my son and I were placed in a room above a pub. The events that took place between Sean and I during that time are hazy in my memory. However, after an altercation with Sean, the council placed me in a women's refuge with two other families. It was a relief not to feel so isolated. After several turbulent months of homelessness, my son and I were finally settled in a new home. Sean and I patched things up, despite all the hurt he had caused, I couldn't stay angry with him for long. But, as before, we found ourselves back on drugs.

Realisation Hits

In my early 20s, I worked part-time in retail while studying for my A-Levels, hoping to secure a place at university. However, heroin was quickly becoming a problem, and soon I found myself using it daily. I had become what you'd call a functioning addict. As time passed, I grew increasingly reclusive. Weekends were no longer spent having fun or socialising, and when my son was with my parents, I would be at home using.

One Sunday morning, I found myself struggling to reach my dealer, withdrawal symptoms hit me with full-force anxiety, sweating, and stomach cramps, nothing I had ever experienced before. I had no idea what was happening to me, I knew I felt shocking, and I needed heroin fast.

That's when the realisation hit me. I was fully addicted. How had this happened? I had always thought I was different, that I could avoid becoming dependent. A false sense of security as I told myself that I was the one in control. Sean had warned me this day would come, but I refused to listen. 'Not me,' I'd tell myself, 'I'll never become dependent.' How naïve I was. Its power was just too great!

To avoid going through that hell again, I started buying larger amounts, stocking up for the week. I couldn't face another agonising Sunday like that. This was not the life I had imagined for myself at all, I had to admit it to myself, I needed help. I reached out to my local drug treatment centre and was placed on a methadone program. I stopped using heroin immediately, though still difficult, life became somewhat more manageable. During this time, I made the difficult decision to end things with Sean.

Temporary Escape

Not long after, I met someone new. He swept me off my feet, showering me with affection making me feel like a princess. It was everything I needed to escape the pain Sean had caused me. What I didn't realise was that I was being love bombed with his excessive attention and praise which disguised a far more manipulative side. He seemed like my knight in shining armour, I mistook his charm for genuine love. Before long, he moved in with me and my son and I became pregnant with my second child. For a while, life felt better, but I was blind to the truth and his narcissistic behaviour.

This relationship brought more pain, I soon discovered he was cheating on me while I was heavily pregnant. After my son was born, more truths began to emerge. I'll admit, I wasn't perfect and retaliated in ways I'm not proud of. Life wasn't going the way I had hoped, and I found myself turning to alcohol to numb the pain swapping one addiction for another. A few months after my son was born, we moved to a new house. But deep down I was extremely miserable, and eventually, I ended the relationship for good.

Love Returns But The Scars Remain

After some time apart, I found myself reconciling with Sean. A few months later, I realised he was the true love of my life. Despite the messiness of our past, we had both grown, especially Sean. By the time we reconnected, he was in his late 20s, and it was clear how much he had matured. It felt right, and we were happy to be back together.

Sean became a fantastic stepdad to my son. I truly believe he saw this as his chance to make amends, and he stepped up in ways I never expected. I feel it couldn't have been easy for him to accept a child who wasn't his. Our love for each other was undeniable, and this was going to be the start of us building a bright future together. Our dream of a perfect life together was shattered in the most devastating way. Sean passed away at the age of 30, just as our son was approaching 9 years old.

The pain I felt was indescribable. Sean was my person the one I thought I would spend the rest of my life with. Just like that, he was gone. It didn't seem real, a sudden and intense retching heartache I wasn't prepared for.

In an effort to cope, I focused on finishing my final year at university. During that time, I made the decision to move house. The place was filled with too many memories of Sean, and I needed a fresh start. One of Sean's friends, Dean offered to help with the move, and we started spending more and more time together. He reminded me of Sean in so many ways, and I enjoyed being in his company. It was comforting and after a short while, we began seeing each other. However this relationship had issues, he was an addict just like me!

A New Beginning, A Familiar End

After graduating with a 2.1 BSc Honours degree, Sean's death hit me harder than ever. I had nothing left to focus on and the emptiness quickly drove me back to what I knew best. In a failed attempt to numb the pain, alcohol, and pills only plunged me deeper into despair. I found myself in a very dark place, and this time, I couldn't pull myself out.

Desperate for change, I turned to the church for help. I spent months taking my children to services every Sunday, I even participated in home visits to study the Bible. But despite my best efforts, it wasn't enough. Before long, I found myself right back where I started, stuck in the same destructive cycle.

Dean and I started using together and despite his best efforts to stop me, I began injecting. Even though he had warned me, injecting led me down a darker path. Shortly after, my life spiralled out of control in the blink of an eye. Within a few months I lost everything, my children moved in with my parents, and Social Services became involved. Eventually, my youngest was placed with a family member after my mum, still grieving the loss of my father, struggled to cope. I found myself with nothing, no home, no family, no job, no stability.

Over time, I managed to clean up. I moved into a new house with my youngest, and for the first time, I dared to believe this could be my opportunity to rebuild my life, however this was short lived.

The Hole You Left Behind

One day, someone from my past triggered me, and I fell back into old coping mechanisms. In a moment of vulnerability, I turned to alcohol while caring for my son. I lost control and yelled at him, something completely out of my character. The following day, he informed school he didn't want to come home that evening. Without attempting to understand and talk to me about it, Social Services took him away. To this day, they never uncovered the full story or why my son said what he did. What's even more frustrating is that, at the time, I wasn't using heroin I was on a methadone program.

And just like that, he was gone. Taken! I would NEVER be able to put into words the amount of pain I experienced during that time. It literally felt like someone ripped my soul out. It was the worst kind of emptiness, deeper than anything I'd ever experienced. My world crumbled in an instant; I didn't want to be here anymore.

I won't go into the gritty details of how I was living when my son was taken, the lack of gas, electricity, and food. How, something as simple as toilet paper became a luxury I couldn't afford. I won't talk about the self-harm or the fact that I was high every single day, with no escape from the madness. I could see no way out, and the chaos of that time could fill an entire chapter on its own. It felt as though my soul had been torn apart. It consumed me entirely, taking over every part of who I was. Each waking second, I was locked in a mental prison. When I did use, there was a brief moment of relief, but it wasn't real comfort. I was simply numb, to the pain, to everything.

In the depths of my addiction, the reality of what I had done to the people I loved hit me with full force. I had caused harm; irreversible damage and I couldn't escape my guilt. My addiction had torn apart the relationships I held most dear, and that weight was unbearable. Every waking moment, I was consumed by the pain I had caused them. The destruction I had brought into their lives followed me like a shadow, one I couldn't outrun.

This wasn't the life I had envisioned for myself. In a moment of pure desperation, I reached out to the one person who had always believed in me, my mom. Despite the pain I had caused her, she was always there when I truly needed support. She never gave up on me, holding onto hope, that one day I would find my way, and break free from my addiction.

After 10 years together I made the difficult decision to leave Dean, as he remained trapped in addiction. I moved in with my mom and, for the first time, fully committed to my recovery. Before I realised it, I had accumulated several months of sobriety. I distanced myself from people, places, and things, that once fuelled my addiction. The urge to use no longer dominated my thoughts, and today, life is a far cry away from what once consumed my entire being.

The Journey
From Pain To Purpose: Awakening The Spirit Within

During this time, I embarked on a deep journey of self-growth. It wasn't easy, and there were many dark nights of the soul, but despite this I kept moving forward. I embarked on a personal development journey; this helped me understand and process the pain and trauma I had carried for so long. Slowly, my perspective began to shift, I no longer saw myself as a junkie trapped in an endless cycle. Instead, I recognised that I had the power to change.

Spending time alone was crucial for my healing. I found an online mentor and eagerly embraced every workshop I could. These experiences brought me a sense of peace and fulfilment, something I had never known before. I learned to love myself and create my own happiness from within. I realised that true happiness doesn't come from external sources, it is something we cultivate within ourselves. With each passing day, the light within me grew stronger, and for the first time in years, I genuinely felt happy. Spiritual practices became the foundation for my transformation.

Through meditation and intentional pauses throughout my day, I trained my mind to reach a new level of consciousness. I began to notice more opportunities and synchronicities; I learned to trust my intuition. Universal downloads started flowing to me, something I had never experienced. I was being guided to train in different healing modalities.

After researching the benefits of sound healing and understanding how different frequencies can promote physical and emotional well-being, I realised how aligned this is with the idea that we are all energy. This insight deeply resonated with me, and I trained in crystal bowl healing, along with other healing modalities, including Reiki. I felt passionate to help others and started my own energy healing business. I offer support to those seeking healing and transformation, helping them align with their life purpose.

The Journey

If my story has inspired or resonated with you, I'd love to connect. Whether you're seeking healing or would like to follow my journey, feel free to reach out through my social media links below. I'm here to support you and would be honoured to be a part of your healing journey.

Since writing my chapter for this book, I now have full time care of my youngest son. I asked him for a quote to go in my chapter and he said 'results not promises' and I think that perfectly sums it up.

You can find me at:

https://www.facebook.com/sharon.bedford.1614

TikTok **@sharbed83**

sharb83@myyahoo.com

Chapter Ten

By Harriet Clay

Healer At Heart

From a young age I knew I was a healer. Even during my primary school years, I would find friends coming to me with their problems, I was a little councillor and really wanted to help. I am 33 now and this hasn't changed, I learned some tough lessons along the way, but I am still here standing to tell the tale. I am now a qualified Reiki master along with other healing modalities and I am going to tell my story of how I overcame a 9-year abusive relationship with my twin's father, no names will be mentioned throughout as there is still an ongoing court case. If one person reading this realises that they deserve more and chooses to put themselves first, I feel I have accomplished what I set out to.

I had an amazing childhood. I am an only child that comes from an incredibly loving, safe, fun family unit. I am very lucky for the upbringing I had and the support I got and still get to this day. I honestly wouldn't change anything about my younger years. My childhood really was carefree, and I was always taught I could come to my parents with anything. This was something that during my teenage years I was immensely grateful for. However bad something was, and things did get bad, I always knew I could confide in my parents and felt safe to do so.

I was diagnosed with depression at the age of 12 and medicated ever since. No one ever stopped and considered the root cause of why I was feeling depressed, and I was just moved from one anti-depressant to the next. It is only now I realise I had hit an Autism/ADHD burnout and daily life and interactions with people were becoming more and more difficult. I spent the majority of my childhood and teenage years trying to fit in and mask who I really was. This led me down certain paths and I put myself in dangerous positions. Somehow, I always came out stronger, even when it didn't feel like it at the time. It was a battle to even get out of bed most mornings.

Relationships were never easy for me. The healer in me would unconsciously always seem to attract broken and unhealed men. For many years all I wanted to do was try to help but I was going about it all wrong and hurting myself in the process. At this stage of my life and my journey I didn't know any better, I wanted to be the one that "changed the bad boy" I guess. I had visions of my happily ever after and from a child I dreamed of a fairy tale wedding. I was searching for my prince charming but in some not very charming men. This was a habit of mine and until I learnt my lesson I was just attracting the same person, in different bodies.

The Monster Behind The Mask

I gave birth to my first daughter when I was 17. I was still young and naive and completely underestimated the pressures of having a baby. My depression really hit, and I struggled to even function. I was incredibly lucky to be still living with my parents and having their support on a daily basis. Things could have taken a bad turn if I hadn't had the support from them. I was still very immature at this stage and didn't know how to deal with my emotions. I found myself trying to numb my feelings any way I could.

I was 19 when I first met my ex-partner and hanging around in the pubs at the weekend while my parents watched my daughter. I wanted to be a normal teenager, even if it was just for one night a week. We had some good nights out together and I really enjoyed his company.

I never wanted the night to end knowing I had to wait until next weekend to see him again. This only lasted a few months because he moved across the country.

A few years passed of not being in contact with him until I got a message completely out of the blue. We started speaking again and things moved fast from there. Within a month or so he had moved back across the country and moved into my little flat with me. At this point I really couldn't be happier, he made me feel special and things were finally starting to look up in my love life.

Little did I know what was unfolding for me. It started with the name calling, he loved to call me fat because he knew I was self-conscience about my weight. Things started off very gradually and then progressively got more verbally abusive as time passed. In the early stages of our relationship, it was a lot more on an emotional level, he would pick away at me until eventually I felt so worthless about myself and how I looked.

If I had made an effort with my appearance he wouldn't so much as even compliment me and tell me I looked nice. At one point I did ask him why this was, because it would really upset me. His answer would be that he found it "easier to say nasty things to people than he did nice things." I actually thought this was really sad and I wanted to try and warm his heart, I guess. As silly as it sounds, its only when I look back now I see how much of a red flag that was, but I didn't see it at the time, or maybe I did and chose to ignore my intuition but I just wanted to make things better.

Things didn't get better in fact they continued to get progressively worse. Why was this happening? All I wanted was to be loved. All I wanted was for him to put his arms around me and give me a big hug and tell me everything was going to be alright. All I got was a blank stare. Did he really hate me that much? I started to think that maybe if I changed things would change. Maybe if I was prettier, he would compliment me. All these things would consume my mind until I couldn't even think straight.

I fell pregnant with twins which we were both happy about and part of me thought that maybe this would bring us together as a team, and when the twins were new-borns, we were getting on and working together well. Unfortunately, this didn't last long as the reality of having two crying babies to deal with was really kicking in. He would constantly moan and complain about the crying, and it would make him agitated. I would find myself constantly having to overcompensate because I was doing it mostly on my own, and feeling completely overwhelmed.

When the twins were about two years old, both the nursery and I picked up on early signs of autism. This was always a problem in his eyes, and he would always refuse to ever listen or do any research regarding autism and understanding his children better. I on the other hand believe knowledge is power, so I was researching everything and wanted to share helpful tips I was picking up with him, but he wasn't interested in the slightest.

It wouldn't be long before the name calling started, "you fat bitch" "look at you" "wobble wobble" wobbling his belly and aiming it at me, the body that had carried his twins safely for 9 months, he really knew what to say to cut me deep. He would get a haunting glare in his eyes, and they would look like they had turned black. He would get a smirk across his face that looked like he was getting pleasure from the pain he was causing me.

His hand grabbed for my throat, twisting my neck and pulling me down onto the floor. He stood back up and I thought maybe I had gotten away lightly. I was frozen in fear when a foot came swinging towards me, the pain was excruciating! I had just been kicked in my stomach below my c section wound, and I cried out in pain I had never experienced before. I was on the floor again, this wasn't the first time this had happened, but never this severe before. I just wanted it all to stop. I stayed laying on the floor for a moment. In the meantime, he got his phone out and took a photo of me laying on the floor. Then I heard him say, "actually maybe that is a bit sick, I should delete that."

I could not believe what had just happened. How could this really be my life? How was I going to make this stop? Then I heard the twins crying in the background and somehow that was enough to snap me out of it. I disassociated from any feelings and had no choice but to look after the twins and carry on like nothing had happened. A few weeks would pass without any arguments. He would make sure to cry and grovel and promise me it would never happen again. But it always happened again. It just continued getting worse. My head and heart were in conflict because even though he was the one hurting me, he was also the one to take the pain away. It was a vicious cycle.

An Earth Angel

At the perfect time I came across the most amazing woman Gemma, who runs an incredible academy for women, called the VIP Manifesting Academy. It was a safe space for ladies who were ready to change their lives. Everything Gemma said really resonated with my soul and hearing her speak would give me goosebumps. I knew there had to be more to life than what I was experiencing at that moment. I feel like Gemma was put in my path just when I needed her to show me how the power of our mind can truly impact our lives. I had never even tried meditation before meeting Gemma, but she truly does the most amazing, guided meditations, which helped me to learn to be still in my own mind and body. The sensation of safety and warmth I would experience throughout was amazing. I would somehow feel lighter and much more relaxed. This was a feeling I wanted to experience more of.

It wasn't always easy to find the time to spend doing my meditation and the mindset activities Gemma would do in the academy. I would be made fun of by my ex and really laughed at for trying to heal myself. Looking back now, of course he didn't want me to start learning to heal, that would make me harder to manipulate.

Gemma was extremely honest with all the ladies in the academy about her past relationship of abuse with a narcissistic ex. This was the first time I ever heard the word narcissist but hearing her story it resonated so much with what I was going through, and I decided to do my own research on narcissism. What I found was truly shocking but also explained a lot.

"A narcissist never wants to discuss their actions, they only want to provoke your reaction, so that your reaction can be used as a distraction from their actions." Read that again!

The Break

Things between me and him weren't always bad. When we were getting along things were great. I felt like he was my best friend as well as my partner, but it would never take long before we were back to square one. I guess I was just holding my breath until the next argument took place, it was like constantly walking on eggshells. I could feel the tension; the twins could feel the tension because they would always be more unsettled, and anyone who entered our home would feel it too. It wasn't a nice place to be, but even though he was the one hurting me and making me cry, he was the one who made me feel whole again afterwards. I was stuck between my head and my heart.

My mental health was decreasing on the daily and I really started to wonder if I was going crazy. Was I the one that was causing all this? He would constantly remind me how hard it was for him to have to live with someone with depression, never taking into consideration what was making me sad. Anytime I tried to express my feelings he would always take it as a dig, and I would be accused of trying to start an argument.

His first reaction in arguments would always be to go for my throat. He thought he wouldn't leave any marks, but little did he know I had been secretly taking pictures of any injuries he had inflicted on me for the past 4-5 years, knowing one day I would finally get the courage to walk away.

There is one occasion that will stay burned in my brain for the rest of my life. He had me around the throat and restrained me on the floor, the grip getting stronger. The look in his eyes, they would turn black, and he would get a sadistic smirk on his face. I couldn't breathe! At this point normally he would get up, but not this time. His grip stayed firm around my neck, and I looked over and could see one of my twins witnessing what was happening. I tried to fight back but I couldn't breathe and had no strength left. I was convinced my little boy was about to watch his mummy die. I had given up. I wasn't fighting back as I had accepted this was my time to die. Then I heard a voice in my head saying, "it's not over, one last push" and I kicked out as hard as I could, managing to untangle myself from his grip. All I wanted to do at this point was gather my twins up and go to the furthest room possible away from him.

The next morning, I decided to try and speak with him and asked, "if someone hurt our daughter like you hurt me last night, how would you feel?" To be honest I was expecting him to say, "well I'd kill them" like you would expect a father to say. But what came out of his mouth was truly shocking, without hesitation he replied, "I would ask her what she did to deserve it." I got shivers throughout my entire body and felt sick to my stomach, I knew in my heart of hearts I needed to get out now, not only for me but for my children.

The Interview Process

Because of the twins suspected autism at this point, every 6 months or so I would be invited into the twin's nursery for a meeting with staff to discuss their progress and any concerns. These meetings were always a good way to touch base and regroup to come up with strategies to help the twin's development going forward. I was absolutely dreading this meeting because I knew I had to be honest with them about what had been going on. The staff were incredible, and the manager made it clear that I had no choice but to report this to the police as it was a serious safeguarding concern regarding the twins and having contact with him. The thought of reporting this all to the police after years of making excuses for the abuse was hard. I didn't see myself as a victim because I was so brainwashed into thinking I deserved what I was getting. I felt like I was betraying him, and it was the hardest thing I have ever had to do.

Speaking with the police was extremely traumatising. I was interviewed by a male officer for starters, and I was in there making a statement for 4 hours. During the interview I had to go through 38 injury images of myself. The police wanted times, dates and even rooms in the house the incidents had occurred in. This was impossible for me to recall due to it being ongoing for over 5 years. Due to the trauma, my brain had shut out a lot of older incidents as a way of protecting me.

Out of the 38 images the police managed to secure 3 charges, 3!! This was because I hadn't reported the offences within the 6-month time limit that the police have on charges of assault and for this reason they couldn't be counted. I was absolutely mortified and felt like I was actually the one being questioned. It takes victims of domestic violence years to find the strength to find their voice, to then be told the injuries don't count because they weren't reported in time.

I am currently going through court for a second time because the charge of controlling and cohesive behaviour was missed. I was let down massively by the police and had no choice but to go through this whole procedure again to get the justice I deserved first time around. My advice to anyone going through a similar situation is to make sure the police have the correct charges secured, the police did admit that mistakes had been made so hopefully lessons were learnt and the next woman won't have to go through the same as I did.

My Story, Someone Else's Survival Guide

I threw myself in completely with my inner healing. I worked closely alongside Gemma, she spoke so authentically, that something clicked in my head. She had been there before and had come out the other side turning her pain into power. This is exactly what I was going to do. There was hope and this was the shining light I needed to pull me out of the dark place. All my life I had been waiting for my knight in shining armour to come and save me, and never in a million years realised that I was the only person who could. I began learning different healing modalities, starting with Reiki level 1, level 2 and now I am a Reiki master teacher.

14/04/23 was the last time my ex laid his hands on me and 14/04/24 exactly one year later I passed my Reiki level 1 qualification. The difference one year can make in your life if you really put your mind to your inner healing and growth is amazing. I am also trained in other healing modalities and have really turned my life around.

The break truly was where the light entered for me, and with help from Gemma I turned my pain into power. I learnt to channel the healer in me in a healthy way. Everything I had been through up until this point was just getting me ready to step into my own power. I had lessons to learn along the way, but I genuinely wouldn't change anything I have been through as it has made me the person I am today, and my story isn't over!

The Journey

A wise woman once told me that the best way to predict your future, is to write it yourself.

To get in touch or ask me anything my contact details are:

Harriet Clay - **https://www.facebook.com/share/1ByKK3ruhY/**

Harriets Healing Hands - **https://www.facebook.com/share/1ACefGZai8/**

TikTok - **https://www.tiktok.com/@harrietshealingha?_t=ZG-8uDB1jwTLKT&_r=1**

Email address - **HarrietsHealingHands@gmail.com**

Feel free to send me a message, I really would love to connect.

Chapter Eleven

By Kelley Crocker

A New Beginning In Mid-Wales

It was 1984 and I was 10 years old. Moving from the city to a small market town marked the beginning of a new chapter—one shadowed by loneliness and confusion leaving behind the close-knit embrace of my mother's family. I found myself in an unfamiliar school, with only my younger brother by my side. The warmth of familiarity was replaced by the cold sting of bullying.

The First Encounters With Cruelty

My first encounter came swiftly. Within a few weeks whilst in Primary school two boys asked me out; when I refused, they punched me after school. I stumbled home, tears blurring my vision, not understanding why my words had invited fists. Later, when older students shared our canteen during renovations, two girls I'd never met singled me out, hurling cruel smutty names that clung to me like shadows. Their words carved deeper wounds than any punch could. As an empath, I absorbed every insult, replaying them until I believed them.

Another time when I was about 12 years old, a boy dragged me across a park by my hair after I declined to be his girlfriend. My dress rode up, jelly shoes lost, knees scraped raw on gravel. Standing barefoot, exposed and powerless after he had run off, I felt the weight of an unspoken lesson: it wasn't safe to be a girl. This was the start of me embodying my masculine side as a protection mechanism.

The Journey

One of the worse things that happened to me was whilst walking along the riverbank where a group of older boys were fishing. I had to pass by them to get home and one of the boys had just caught an eel. He chopped the head off and put the body down the back of my top. Whilst all the others laughed, I was distraught with fear, feeling this thing wriggling against my skin, covered in blood. To this day if I see an eel, it gives me an eerie feeling.

When my brother was just 10 years old there was this older boy, around 14, known for getting into trouble. One day he punched my brother for no reason calling him names, leaving him in tears. Seeing my brother like that ignited something in me. I told him, "Come on, we're going to find him, and you're going to stand up for yourself." We found the boy hiding in the girl's toilet with two girls I knew. I grabbed him and shoved him into a cubicle, and he hit his back against the metal toilet roll holder.

He was completely caught off guard. Holding him with all my strength, I shouted for my brother to hit him, but he froze, fear written all over his face. Suddenly, the boy punched me so hard on the side of my head that my ears rang, and my head throbbed. For a moment, it felt like everything went silent, and time slowed down. But in that moment, all the rage and hurt I had been carrying over the past 2 years erupted. I fought back with everything I had, throwing punch after punch between his strikes. Eventually, he slipped past me and ran out of the toilet. After that day, he never laid a hand on my brother again. He never even dared to speak to me. That experience taught me the strength I had within myself, not just to protect my brother, but to stand up against anyone who tried to bully or intimidate us.

Defending My Brother, Defending Myself

Defending my brother became my mission, even when fear gripped.

I fought not just for him, but against the growing belief that we were inherently flawed. Why were people in this town treating us like this? Food became my refuge and his; we had easy access to it as my parents owned a bakery and café. My excess weight was a shield against emotions too heavy to carry. The weight I gained was armour, my body's way of saying, "You can't hurt me." My subconscious certainly did its job of keeping me safe. Every bite was numbing down the negative feelings I was feeling. I realised if I was bigger and stronger I could fight back.

I hated school even though I was bright and had the ability to do well. Daily there was some type of jibes which just made me even more self-loathing. I had become paranoid if someone looked at me, I would think they were saying things about me taking the mickey. I would stutter if the English teacher asked me to read out to the class as I was so nervous, I just could not get my words out, the adrenaline would be felt and I could feel my heart racing. If my name was picked to read a hymn is assembly, I would take the day off sick begging my mum not to send me to school. I even wrote my own notes. At one time we had the truancy officer speaking to my mum, there were no fines in my school days, but it was still not nice for that to be brought to my mums' attention.

I never told my parents about the bullying. I feared my father's reaction more than the bullies blows, he would have been straight around to the parents houses and would have probably hit their fathers trying to protect me. I was carrying that burden of fighting life alone and also trying to protect my dad. Silence became my strategy, anger my defence. I grew into someone who fought first and questioned later, mistaking rage for strength. Compliments felt like traps; vulnerability, a weakness I couldn't afford. I felt people were disingenuous, having some ulterior motive by being nice to me.

In that early part of my life, I was lost in a maze of negative beliefs. At one point I did not want to be here, feeling so alone, misunderstood, unloved. I felt so disconnected from my body that I hated it and as the years rolled on, I bullied myself internally. I think in a certain way this was because I believed those who had bullied me so much in my formative years. My mum and dad were at times emotionally unavailable to me as they were busy. All my physical needs were met but you must have both from your parents to be able to process those emotions that were felt at the time to close the trauma loop.

Searching For Freedom, Carrying The Wounds Into Adulthood

In my early twenties, I left that town, thinking freedom was a new place. But I carried my burdens with me—low self-esteem, a poor body image, and a heart seeking love in all the wrong places. I became a perfectionist, chasing achievements to mask my insecurities. My independence became a fortress, impenetrable and isolating. Relationships were mirrors reflecting my unhealed wounds, filled with emotional unavailability and co-dependency.

I worked in male dominated jobs, showing I was as good as them, as strong as them, as skilled as them. It wasn't until years later, through spiritual awakening and profound loss, that I saw the truth: the cruelty I endured wasn't a reflection of me but of those who inflicted it. Healing meant facing my shadow, shedding layers of pain, and rediscovering the worth that had been mine all along. When I look back at those who did the bullying, they had dysfunctional families, absent mothers and fathers. I was an easy target until I took the steps to stand up for myself.

My whole life I have stuck up for people, jumping in where angels have feared to tread. I have championed the underdog whether in a work situation with a bullying boss or amongst colleagues or friends. I would voice my distaste that what they were doing was wrong and let them know that the way they were behaving was unacceptable.

I would be known as intimidating stepping in straight away, and I suppose I was on the defence in situations before anyone had a chance to do anything to me. I promised myself no one would bully me in any type of situation again in my life. This was not my intention, but I was righteous always seeking the truth and having high expectations for people to act with integrity as I always did. My word was my honour. I disliked anyone who was false and being an empath and always having to be hyper vigilant I could tell by people's body language that they were not being genuine.

The Turning Point: A Spiritual Awakening

The turning point came at forty years old after the end of a significant relationship. It pushed me into a spiritual awakening, a journey inward rather than outward. I could see for the first time the patterns I had been repeating. I had learned about my attachment style of being trauma bonded, by being an anxious attached person, always needing constant communication, being hypervigilant, and extremely jealous of the person I was with. This came from a place of fear defending the love that I felt for the person I was with at the time, mistrusting if they did actually love me. This leads to trying to maintain that relationship at any cost because you cannot bear to feel rejected or abandoned, because this reinforces your belief that you are not good enough or loveable enough.

This type of attachment style will only attract an avoidant attached person who by their own trauma will feel trapped, always thinking they can find a better person, and fearing being controlled. So, if questioned about how they know someone they take this the wrong way as if you are accusing them of doing something instead of trying to feel safe by knowing how they know that person. They withdraw when overwhelmed and are quick to find reasons to leave so they fear commitment which is an absolute nightmare for the other type of person.

During that relationship, I saw my shadow side and I also saw his shadow side and narcissistic traits. No one can fix this outside of yourself you have to be willing to go deep and heal those inner wounds. Call it ego, or inner child. I felt rejected by him but deep down I had rejected myself and had settled with someone who was not worth my time or energy and because of feeling unloved I clung onto that familiar hurt.

The subconscious would rather keep you in a familiar hell than to expend energy letting go of the fear to try something else that would make your life better, as it's a creature of habit. This is how it survives and keeps you stuck in those negative patterns. I started to hear voices to go to the spiritual church that I had passed by for 15 years and started to notice angel numbers 1111, 333, 444, 1212, 555 all the time. I would think of something and then it would appear like a book or program or a person who had spiritual connections, so my world was opening up to understand myself more and why we behave the way we do.

A chance meeting with a clairvoyant in a dance hall led me to receive Reiki healing, where, lying on that couch, tears I didn't know I'd buried surfaced. It was a release of years of self-loathing, grief, and suppressed emotions. I trained to Master Teacher level as I knew this would be part of me, I was part of something universal, there was so much abundance available to me if I could move forward and clear the past hurts. My final attunement to the energies after a 5-day residential course in Glastonbury was during a profound ceremony at Stonehenge, where I felt really connected to spirit with a group of amazing like-minded souls.

THE JOURNEY
Healing Through Spiritual Growth

My journey didn't stop with Reiki. I spent six years studying in a spiritual church, exploring various healing modalities tuning into my own intuition as well as my spiritual guides. It was a place I finally felt at home with people who understood the universal bigger picture. Learning and reading up on everything I could to be able to be the best person to aid someone else to heal their lives.

In 2023 I discovered Belief Coding ® a transformative practice that helps heal the root causes of painful negative experiences and trauma. A modality that is science backed using all the best from existing techniques but has been proven to go deeper than hypnosis. The founder Jessica Cunnigham continually works hard to evolve our practices to reach even deeper aspects of ourselves for those to have profound everlasting shifts. I went to the in-person training in Sheffield as I felt so drawn to it. I have worked on myself and have received facilitations from others to clear lots of those painful experiences from my past that I have mentioned earlier.

Now if my mind wonders back to them, they are just neutral and have no impact on me emotionally or physically because I gave little Kelley what she needed at the time and was able to go back to the painful memory and reframe the emotions to feel better and to believe positive new beliefs. The biggest aspects to heal were that it was not safe to lose the weight not only emotionally but physically. All these years I had an unconscious fear if I did lose the weight, I would not be able to defend myself physically, it was not safe to be feminine, it was not safe to feel attractive as this drew the wrong attention towards me. I did not believe I deserved those things for me to allow myself to soften and be at peace with myself as I always expected to be hurt by the next person. I have been fighting that internally for all these years and manifesting people and jobs that validate those beliefs. That is what the brain does it brings those experiences to you because you are thinking that way and have done for so long.

Facing Darkness, Finding Light

Yet, healing wasn't linear. I faced a few dark nights of the soul, grappling with profound loss when my father and brother passed away just 11 weeks apart. Grief peeled back layers of anger and hurt, revealing empathy and understanding. I saw beyond my pain to the struggle's others carried, recognising that hurt people often hurt people. I understood that as souls we come here for that human experience and walk with other souls in our soul clusters everyone playing their part just at the right time for us to learn, grow and evolve.

A dark night of the soul is where you experience a spiritual or emotional crisis where you feel profound doubt, despair, or a sense of disconnection from meaning, purpose, or the divine. It felt like a period of inner emptiness or darkness, where all my previous beliefs or comforts no longer provided solace. I just felt so alone again. I just survived for months getting up going to work and coming back home but I underwent deep growth, shedding old attachments, letting go of the ego that had been keeping me safe and emerging with greater clarity, faith, and self-awareness. I had shed my skin and had awakened to the truth, my truth. I am who I am now, and I do not care what anyone thinks of me. I am authentic and nothing or no one can change that as my belief in myself is so strong.

Embracing Wholeness

Through spiritual growth, I confronted my shadow, acknowledged my inner child, and understood that my value was never tied to others' perceptions. I no longer sought validation externally. Instead, I embraced my imperfections, set boundaries, and found peace in authenticity. The little girl who once felt invisible had finally found her voice, her strength rooted not in anger but in self-love and acceptance.

The Journey

Throughout my life, I remain a caring, kind person, never judging others but dedicating my life to helping them break free from their wounds and limiting beliefs. My empathic nature, once a source of pain, became my greatest gift. My life's path and work now is to help others find that same light within themselves to heal, to grow, and to understand that they are whole, just as they are. Either through Advanced Belief Coding, Pellowah and Reiki healing. I am working on combining everything I have learned to create a program to help those with weight issues from past trauma via the subconscious mind.

I am still a spiritual seeker and will always learn as a soul in this incarnation until I pass back to spirit and my time has ended. My lasting words to anyone who reads this chapter would be you have the power within to heal anything and everything, we can rewrite our stories we tell ourselves that were formed in our youth, all the cultural and societal beliefs we pick up that are not ours to believe. We all have so much potential and whilst the medical model can help people, I would always suggest to research the possibilities of alternative therapies to help you become the best version of yourself. Seek to reconnect to that inner child, tell him or her that they are loved and make it your life's mission to always be the parent that they never had. Find the truth within. Do not look outside yourself for the answers. Understand you are a child of the divine, ignite that spark within. Keep that flame burning brightly as you move through the stages of your life. You are never too old to learn, grow and evolve this is your birth right. If you are interested in my services then please contact me as below.

All my love your soul sister x

https://www.linkedin.com/in/kelley-crocker-advanced-bc

Chapter Twelve

By Nat Simpkin

This Is Me!!!

It's taken me 40 years to finally find myself and my life's purpose. So here I am, now a 40-year old single mum to 2 beautiful miracles. On another journey to becoming self-employed after finding my calling to healing, not just for myself but others too. So here is a little bit of my story in the hope that it could help you navigate yours.

The Beginning And Growing Up

Little did I know that trauma could start as far back as to when you're in the womb (it can be further back, but that's for another story) but yes, that's where mine started. My "mother", I use that term loosely, found out she was pregnant not long after her best friend. Neither of them chose to know the sex of the baby, but deep down even though I was far from planned my "mother" wanted me to be a boy. In the last trimester her friend called with the news she had just had a boy.

My "mother" was devastated as she instantly knew the mistake inside her was a girl. The story goes that not long after I apparently kicked her and got my foot lodged in her rib cage which didn't dislodge until she was in labour with me which was four weeks over my due date. I was born with a slight heart murmur and a deformity to my right foot, which has and still does cause problems.

Growing up was tough and death introduced itself when I was only two when my sister was born sleeping. I can still remember being dropped off at my grandmother's house, then going to the hospital and looking everywhere for the baby.

I also knew I was different from a young age. I could sense things, see things and just know things. For example, I would see people walking through my bedroom at night-time, and then when I was 7, I saw a beautiful little girl of about 3 years old, she was dancing in front of the fireplace at a salon as I was having my ears pierced. But when I mentioned her no one could see her but me.

Then another time I was at a toy stall at the market. The owner showed a beautiful bride doll all in white and asked if anyone could guess what the other dress colours were. They were all in sealed boxes, and I pointed to each one and told him what each dress colour was. His face was a picture as he was opening them, he then turned to my dad and said, "she's a psychic mate."

My parents didn't get on, so I grew up rather quickly trying to shield my younger sister from what was going on. Then there was my mother's first attempt at overdosing. Finally, they split up when I was around 7, so now I became a yo-yo going from one house to another until the age of 8 when I got thrown across a pub by my mother's then boyfriend just because I moaned due to being tired from school. I returned to my dad's, which was incredibly difficult as it meant being separated from my younger sister. My sister, after a few years, ended up back with me at Dads house, but then history repeated itself. When I was 13, I had no choice but to leave due to day-to-day struggles for my dad then being taken out on me. Then came my adventure finding love.

Trauma Of Love

I met my first love when I was 19, he was 33 and we had nearly 12 years together. It wasn't easy and in six months of being together, the violence started, but I was young and stupid, and I stayed. During this time, I also struggled with not being able to get pregnant. It was the one thing I'd always wanted, to become a mum, but I didn't want to go for tests because I personally believed that to discover that I couldn't have children would have driven me to end my life. So, I just carried on and even though sometimes I would go three months with no period, I couldn't bring myself to test to see yet another negative.

My partner already had children, so we were both 100% certain the problem was with me, so we went on the journey of having fur babies instead, each one of my cats were my sons. I lost one early on because of a heart condition and then my next boy passed a few years later and left a great big gaping hole in my heart. I was heartbroken, but people don't understand as to them he was just a cat.

A week later I then got a call to say my granddad had passed away, I was in complete bits again and then I started smelling pickled onions. I just knew it was my granddad, he always used to make pickled onion and cucumber, and it gave me some peace that I knew he was still with me and that everything wasn't blocked from my childhood. A week before his funeral, I felt like I needed to do something and that night in dream state, I met with my granddad, and we came up with a poem that was personal to him. I woke, grabbed a pen, and word for word, wrote what we had come up with. The day of his funeral I couldn't feel him around me, and I was panicking. I wasn't the kind of person to be seen and have all eyes on me. I walked round to the back of the hearse and asked him to show me a sign he was with me and give me the courage to stand up in front of everyone. They pulled him out and as they were walking past me, a gush of wind came from nowhere and blew his salvation army flag straight off his coffin and into my arms.

My relationship was still up and down but I also had a relationship with his children now, so we decided to get married finally and our wedding date was set for our 11 year anniversary. Two weeks before the wedding I ended up having a can smashed into my face and then when I tried to protect myself, he used my fist against me. But still because of the good times outweighing the bad I went through with the wedding but on the condition that if he ever hurt me again in any way, I would be gone. Eight months later, I left.

I promised myself that no man would ever hurt me again. But again, in a new relationship I found myself with history repeating itself. There were warning signs in the first six months, but I was blind, then came the first time. I was in complete bits that this had happened again and then to have him crying and apologising because he knew what I had already been through. The apologies soon turned into another beating, then another to the point I ended up having a breakdown at work.

My manager took me aside for a chat and told me I needed to seek some help. I cried so much with him talking about things and I was also more emotional because I was also late for my period. It turned out that in one of the worst times of my life was when I finally got what I've always wanted, I was pregnant. I was so scared because I was pregnant for every one of those beatings, but I still stayed, I wanted my child to have the family I never did.

At 28 weeks pregnant, I found myself pinned up against the wall, covered in hot chocolate, and had a knife to my throat. I don't know what happened, he went off like a switch, no warning, nothing and the only reason I called the police was because he threatened to kill himself. The police arrested him, and they pressed charges and took photos of my neck as evidence as I had a gash across my neck that was bleeding.

The day after they released him, I was told I had to vacate the house because the conditions of his parole were that he couldn't be around me. My life was being turned upside down and being ruled by other people and so I ran away. I found myself by a little bridge overlooking the water. The weather was really rough that night and the water was going so fast, and I just didn't want to be here anymore. What would it be like bringing this little girl into this world? Then she kicked me, and I just knew that whatever happened everything would be okay. There was never any more physical violence after that, it was all mental and emotional. In his words, I was a mess, and no one would ever want me. This was being said as he towered over me whilst I was breastfeeding his newborn child.

Time For Single Life

I finally mustered up the courage when my daughter was one to say no more. I didn't want her to grow up like I did and although I wanted her to have the family I didn't, I couldn't let her grow up around the abuse. So, I became homeless with a one-year-old sleeping on sofas and floors until after eight months I finally got a house.

I fell pregnant in 2019 and then lockdown hit, so when you need people around you with being a single mum to a now 3-year-old and pregnant, I was alone. My second little miracle was born, and he was in and out of hospital, which was heart-breaking being away from my daughter.

During lockdown, we received the news that my grandma was being moved to a nearby nursing home due to a decline with her dementia and we finally set a date to be able to do a window visit in September 2020. I couldn't wait to see her as we were very close. I missed her so much and I couldn't wait to introduce her to her new great grandson and so she could see my daughter again. Four days before our visit, baby in hand, I got a knock on the door and knew instantly that she was no longer with us.

Spiritual Awakening

After losing my grandma, I felt lost and guilty for not seeing her, despite not being allowed, and I carried that guilt for years. Everything was just going wrong. The kids and I were constantly poorly and then a friend suggested I cleanse my house. That was the moment my life changed. The 1st of February 2023 I cleansed my house for the first time and as I finished the last room, I can only describe as a surge of energy passing through me. I instantly burst into tears as it felt such a release, but whatever it was also felt like gratitude. That day opened me up to a whole new world. I started feeling and sensing energy more. But with that also came headaches when I was around certain people, ringing in the ears, nose bleeds, problems with my vision, everything was so heightened, and I got worried thinking something was going wrong with me. I went to the doctors, and they sent me for an MRI.

Whilst waiting I was doing lots of research because it's not something you can just talk to anyone about, and I was told the ringing in my ears was a spirit trying to communicate, it was just finding a way to do it. So, I started listening and being more aware of everything. Someone had gifted me a new pack of cards, and as I was cleansing them, I was thinking of my granddad, these were native spirit cards, and he was very into native American Indians. My ears started going off on a certain card so I asked if I should look at it and my ears went off again, it was the grandfather sky card.

I felt so honoured my granddad had come through. Then one day my ears went absolutely crazy, and I didn't know what to do. I can remember shouting, "I can't hear you there's too much noise" and I put my fingers in my ears. I was then drawn to close my eyes, and the next minute my grandma was in front of me. I had no control over my body, tears literally streamed down my face, her lips moved but I didn't hear what she said. Instead, I felt every word and from that day on I never felt any guilt.

Journey Of Healing

I realised that the thing that had been missing in my life was in fact me. I had to get to rock bottom to realise this and start my self love journey and fully discover who I was. I even started having visions of a past life that then a good friend brought into this reality by taking pictures.

It was then I saw the beautiful Gemma Elizabeth Williams advertise the silver Violet flame practitioner course. I have never been so drawn to something so strongly before. I had my attunement and my 21 days healing started and oh my goodness, what a purge it was. I ended up on antibiotics and steroids again as I was feeling so poorly from the release. I'd had so many courses this past year for my asthma and recurrent chest infections.

It was then I decided to attend a sister circle healing session. During my healing session, I saw my past self from my previous vision being freed. Before, my vision showed myself and my children all in white dancing in the woods; after capturing that image on film, what happened next followed. After our dancing in the woods, we made our way back to a very small cottage, so small it was one room for everything. That night a noise woke me, I then saw men around the bed slitting my children's throats before mine. That version of me explained a lot of how I was in this lifetime, scared- scared to be seen and protective of my kids. So, in my healing journey I had not only healed myself but my past self.

It was then I picked up a deck of cards and wanted to take the plunge of reading for others. I helped run a single parent's group on Facebook and asked if anyone would like a reading in exchange for feedback and so I could build up my confidence. That opened the spirit world up even more to me as I then didn't feel scared, so I welcomed them during my card readings.

The one that always sticks with me and made me know this was so very real (I have permission to share) was for a lovely lady. After her reading was over a female came through, this lady was her moms friend. This lady then pushed another female forward telling her it was okay and telling me that it was this beautiful lady's mom. I asked if her mum had passed, and she confirmed. The next minute her mom was showing me her last moments and saying thank you to her daughter for pulling a blanket over her as she was cold, she then sent her love and was gone. My heart was so full and grateful to be able to pass this message on but also hurt because I felt the pain it also brought up for this lovely lady.

Today

As of today, February 2024, I haven't had any antibiotics or steroids for over a year. I've also not needed any of my medication for my asthma for over 6 months as I'm not suffering with it anymore. Every day is a new day to learn and heal and I'm continuing my journey to do more healing courses so I can become self-employed sometime this year and be able offer people as much as I can. I'm now a Reiki master, silver Violet flame Master, crystal healing practitioner, Angelic reiki plus many more.

I'm loving my journey but I'm not going to lie it can be tough. You lose people around you but that's just a part of growing and ascending. You also enjoy solitude more as this is the time you can go within, but no matter the loss it's so rewarding knowing and seeing your own personal growth.

If I could give any advice on things that have helped me, it would be this:

Number one is to remember who you are. You are so much stronger than you think and even if it gets really tough just remember you are needed in this world even if at the time you don't realise it.

Number two is to breathe. I'm not talking about the everyday breathing of in and out. I'm talking about closing your eyes, standing still, feeling that breath go through your nose, into your chest, feeling your tummy expand, holding it there then slowly releasing. That moment of bringing your full awareness to yourself and your body then takes you away from anything that is happening, and when you come back round you can see things a little more clearly. This is really good when you're in fight or flight mode.

Number three is to learn to love yourself and see how much you are worth. This is so important because who doesn't want love? But the power of loving yourself is so magical because then you believe in yourself more. Just remember that you are strong, you are amazing, you are worthy, and you are loved.

How To Find Me

If you feel drawn to me and would like any healings or readings doing, these can all be done distantly as well, so it doesn't matter where in the world you are, remember energy travels. So, here's how to find me:

Facebook group: **Willow's Crystal Moon**

https://www.facebook.com/groups/699825504992916/?ref=share

Email: **Willowscrystalmoon@yahoo.com**

Chapter Thirteen

By Deanne Millis

About Me And My Business

Hi, my name is Deanne Millis, and I am 32 years old. I wanted to write about a part of my life that I have struggled with. I have many lifelong health conditions with a recent diagnosis that has had a massive impact on my life mentally, physically and emotionally. In sharing my story, I hope to help others in a similar position and demonstrate how a positive mindset can change everything including your mind, body, and soul. In doing so, I am able to juggle two successful businesses – Crystalized Boutique and Inner Peace Healings Holistic Therapies whilst being a single mother to a handsome son who also has additional needs.

Living With Ongoing Health Issues

Imagine feeling exhausted all the time no matter how much sleep you've had. That has been my whole life. My sleep apnoea started far before I even realised I had it. At a very young age, I knew something wasn't right. My whole body would hurt all the time, and I had extreme brain fog which impacted my memory and concentration. I also suffered from depression and anxiety and had other symptoms such as severe abdominal pain and extremely painful periods. After visiting the GP, in my late twenties, I was diagnosed with fibromyalgia, endometriosis and polycystic ovaries. I had to have a laparoscopic surgery to identify and remove endometrial tissue which caused the pain to subside for a few years. However, in early 2024, after getting severe contraction like cramps, my GP discovered that not only had the endometriosis come back but I have pelvic varices which was causing the contraction like pain.

In 2024, I underwent a sleep study test where I had to wear a watch to record my brain waves, the oxygen levels in my blood, my heart rate and my breathing while I slept. I was shocked to hear that the findings of this test showed that I have severe sleep apnoea. I remember the consultant telling me I stopped breathing in my sleep 35 times every hour while I was asleep. I even questioned to myself 'how am I even alive?' They told me I have to wear a CPAP machine to help me breathe at night while I'm asleep for the rest of my life. It was definitely a lot to take in and was a massive life change for myself and for my family. My health conditions are one of the reasons for my spiritual journey because my physical health negatively impacted me and my mental health, and to be honest I hit rock bottom.

Having this recent diagnosis I have realised I have managed to be extremely positive about how I dealt with the news which in turn helped me be more positive about how I manage my massive life change. I researched my past diagnoses and have realised I've had sleep apnoea my whole life. Upon reviewing my symptoms, I realised I had put it down to having fibromyalgia and being a typical hormonal teenager.

Living with all these health conditions has been very difficult. I felt like one by one they have taken over my life. On the outside I look normal and healthy. No one would look at me and think anything was wrong with me. It has been frustrating as friends, family and even medical professionals didn't think anything was wrong either. Living with fibromyalgia alone was a struggle for me as some days were better than others. Waking up in the morning was the worst for me every day. I felt awful, so groggy, I couldn't function at all. I felt like The Walking Dead. It was absolutely horrible. Family wouldn't even speak to me in the morning until I spoke to them because it seriously affected my mood.

The Journey

I felt like living with fibromyalgia and sleep apnoea destroyed my health. I felt completely exhausted all the time and struggled day to day. When I had my son, he was my reason to keep going, to keep fighting. No matter how hard things get, my son will always be my why, my fight, he needs me, and no matter what or how old he gets, I will be there for him.

From a very young age, I always longed to be a mum. I have always wanted four children, however trying to conceive was very hard for me. I had multiple miscarriages, which of course, hit me really hard. After discussing my concerns and my recent miscarriages with my doctor, I was then referred to a fertility specialist. At the end of 2017, I found out I was pregnant again and in September 2018, my handsome son Kalleb was born. I was so in love; he was absolutely perfect.

In 2020, my son was diagnosed with autism. I knew something was wrong as I have worked with children for many years and my son wasn't meeting his milestone development. His diagnosis came not long after his first birthday. Kalleb is pre-verbal and needs my full attention as he puts everything in his mouth and is extremely active. His needs are very high, and he needs my support always. He is my absolute world, and I will do anything to support him.

With all my health conditions and having my son with his needs, I needed to get in a better place as my mental health started to deteriorate. I was in a bad place and that's when my spiritual journey began. I started to focus on getting my mental health in a better place not only for myself but also for my son. I was introduced to a group on Facebook called The Vip Manifesting Academy created by Gemma Elizabeth Williams and I haven't looked back. With Gemma's help, I have been able to have a more positive outlook in life, manifest all the wonderful things I have received so far, step out of my comfort zone, focus on meditating more, and I've taken a few accredited courses to help myself and others who may also be on a holistic journey.

I'd be lying if I said it has been easy. Every day you have to work on yourself, especially when you have had a negative mind-set for so long, but you should never give up. Some days can be harder than others. There are always going to be challenges in life and some days you may have a wobble, but as long as you get back up and get back on track that's what matters. As words are spells, it's important to cancel, clear and delete all negative thoughts.

In learning this through my manifesting mentor Gemma Elizabeth Williams, I have been working on my inner self and have seen massive improvements in my mindset and how I deal with negative situations. Some days are trickier than others, but I always get back up, and reset through self-healing such as meditations, a daily gratitude practice, journaling, spiritual healing, exercise, positive affirmations, breath work and rest when needed.

Healing yourself is extremely important and I love that I can do that with all the courses I have done. It can improve your mental and physical health; it can also help with alleviating stress and any other challenges. Working on myself has helped me massively and is still a work in progress but I know now I'm on the right path to become a better version of myself.

The Unseen Journey

Throughout my childhood I have always struggled. I felt different and I found it difficult to fit in with others resulting in social anxiety. Being in constant pain every day and dreading the next. Going out with family or friends would become difficult at times due to pain or being too exhausted. When I'm at my worst I've had to cancel plans with family or friends. It took over my life and put me in a very low point which in turn caused my mindset to become extremely negative.

The Journey

When you're in constant pain every day and exhausted, you don't want to do anything, so your daily routine becomes a struggle. To help me on a day-to-day basis, I adopted the twelve spoon theory. The twelve spoon theory is a metaphor that helps people with fibromyalgia and other chronic illnesses understand how their energy levels are limited. It's a way to explain how people with chronic conditions need to manage their energy and prioritise tasks.

Each task requires a certain number of spoons. For example, getting dressed might take one spoon, while cooking might take three or four. When a person's spoons are used up, they have no more energy for other tasks. On days with more pain, even small tasks might require more spoons. Remember you only have 12 spoons.

Benefits from the Twelve spoon theory can help people with fibromyalgia make informed choices about how to use their energy. It can help people understand the challenges of living with a chronic illness. It can help loved ones and others understand and empathise with people with fibromyalgia.

Different strategies for managing energy-

- Using stools for standing tasks like cooking, showering, or cleaning.

- Planning a day of rest each week.

- Batch cooking on low-pain days.

- Keeping food close to your bed on days when you have low energy.

- Saying "no" when needed.

The Journey

Most people start the day with an unlimited number of possibilities and energy to do whatever they wish, especially young people. For the most part they do not need to worry about the effects of their actions. For most of my life, I have used spoons living with a chronic illness. Since most people who suffer with a chronic illness feel a "loss" of a life they once knew. If I was in control of taking away the spoons, then imagine what it feels like to have someone or something else, in this case Fibromyalgia.

The difference in being sick and being healthy, when you are healthy you expect to have a never-ending supply of "spoons." But when you have to now plan your day, you need to know exactly how many "spoons" you are starting with. It doesn't guarantee that you might not lose some along the way but at least it helps to know where you are starting from. I've wanted more "spoons" for years and haven't found a way yet to get more. Always be conscious of how many spoons you have and do not drop them because you can never forget you have fibromyalgia.

Think about all of the daily tasks you have to do, each one of them will cost you a spoon. Choose your tasks wisely as once your "spoons" are gone, they are gone. You can't just get up. You have to wake up feeling extremely exhausted, groggy, and disoriented. You're unable to function properly, you have to shower every morning just to feel some sort of normal, take away a spoon that just cost you.

You didn't sleep well the night before, you have to crawl out of bed, and then you have to make your self something to eat before you can do anything else. If you don't you can't take your medicine, and if you don't take your medicine, you might as well give up all your spoons. Take away another spoon. You haven't even got dressed yet. You cannot simply just throw clothes on when you are sick.

You have to choose the rest of your day wisely since when your "spoons" are gone, they are gone. Sometimes you can borrow against tomorrow's "spoons" but just think how hard tomorrow will be with less "spoons." I also need to explain that a person who is sick always lives with the looming thought that tomorrow may be worse. So, you do not want to run low on "spoons," because you have no idea when you will truly need them.

I found it tough when I felt like I wasn't being heard by my GP. When explaining my symptoms to my doctor, I was told it was 'just' my fibromyalgia and my son's needs for why I felt the way I did. The difference between being sick and being healthy is having to make choices or consciously think about things when the rest of the world doesn't have to. The healthy have the luxury of a life without choices, a gift most people take for granted.

Looking back on my childhood memories, when I used to stay at my best mate's house, she would joke about me snoring. I thought she was joking around, and I remember telling myself 'I can't be that bad'. My partner would make comments about my snoring too, but I used to think he was trying to wind me up and have a joke with me. They both complained I snored worse when I was unwell. I've now realised that the sleep apnoea was the reason for my snoring.

Going out on car journeys is a struggle for me, especially long ones. I struggle with pain and exhaustion. I wouldn't like to fall asleep because when I wake back up, I'd feel even worse than when I did before I fell asleep. I hated to sit down because of the tiredness that would hit me. I'd just want to go to sleep and not move. I rarely sat down for too long which caused vicious cycles with my health conditions.

Since having my son, I've been trying my very best for him and trying to get the best support for his needs. I manage all the appointments for my son. I got him into a wonderful specialist school which he absolutely loves going to and I also ensure he gets the correct treatments and medications. Before getting my diagnosis, I found everything very overwhelming, but now as I have more of an understanding of my conditions, this has helped me to be in a better place not only physically, but mentally as well.

Isolated And Unseen: The Weight Of No Support

Having these illnesses have definitely made me feel alone. I struggled with my mental health massively. Due to having a chronic illness and sleep apnoea I struggled to be sociable. I was lost, and I didn't know who I was anymore. It becomes a vicious cycle with being in extreme pain, exhaustion and isolation. I went to many appointments feeling unheard, waited months and months to be seen, and struggled with all my symptoms while raising my son who was diagnosed with autism and more recently ADHD. This has impacted my health as my son doesn't sleep very well, which then in turn impacts my sleeping pattern. I have been put on multiple opioids, to help with pain which unfortunately comes with a lot of side effects. I felt trapped. I either have to take the medication and live with the side effects or refuse the medication and live with the pain.

That's why I'm starting to look into the more natural approach and wean myself off all these medications which aren't doing my body any good. In trying the herbal approach alongside the right treatments, I'm slowly starting to feel like myself again and will only improve as I carry on with the treatments and future appointments. I am just grateful that I have the answers and can work on myself even more, and now can step out of my comfort zone, creating the dream life I have dreamed of and give the best I can for my son and family.

Working With Health Conditions

Due to my health conditions, I have been out of work. Since I had my son, I always told myself that I wouldn't let any illness control my life and push through. I wanted to work for myself. I have loved baking and started my own cake business called D Sweet Treats. I did this for about a year and a half, but due to my son needing me at all times, I decided to stop as I couldn't do it anymore. That's when I created Crystalized Boutique. I have always loved crystals, but I started my collection when my mum got me a set and loved them.

So, I thought, why not start my own business selling something I love? Working with crystals and wearing them has really helped me on my journey. I have done crystal markets, which I love doing, too. Stepping out of my comfort zone has been a massive challenge for me, but last year, I pushed myself and completed a number of courses with Gemma Elizabeth Williams.

I have done Reiki Level One, Two and Masters, Angel Reiki, Unicorn Reiki, Crystal Healing, Golden Flame Healing, Rose Quartz Healing, Silver Violet Flame Healing and Mary Magdalene and the Red Rose. I am also doing more courses this year. My Goal this year is to step out of my comfort zone and launch my business, Inner Peace Healings Holistic Therapies, healing others with beautiful Spiritual healing modalities such as Reiki, Crystal Healing, Golden Flame Healing, and all the courses I mentioned above. I will be training in other healing modalities this year, such as Oracle Card Reader, Master Quartz Healing, Amethyst Healing, Ancestral Healing Practitioner, Crystal Reiki Masters, and am looking forward to future courses with Gemma Elizabeth Williams. I can't wait to share all these beautiful healing modalities with the world.

My Advice

Listen to your body. Only you know how you feel and don't let anyone tell you otherwise. Even if you get a diagnosis and feel it may be something else, get a second or third opinion if needed. Doctors can get things wrong. For anyone reading this- if you have a family member, friend, or sibling with any of these conditions or any other health conditions, I ask you to support them the best way you can. It really can become a lonely, isolating place living with ongoing medical conditions that affect your daily life. It's soul destroying having to rediscover yourself. That's why spiritual healing is so important every day, working on yourself, healing yourself within.

Any challenges or trauma in life can make you out of spiritual alignment. Spiritual alignment is the connection between a person and higher source of power or intelligence. It can involve discovering your values and the essence of who you are. This can cause certain health conditions in life so it's important to heal from within even if it takes time. "Rome wasn't built in a day," and "Big journeys begin with small steps." It does not matter how slowly you go, as long as you do not stop! You have got this. Never give up.

If you would like reach out you can connect with me on:

Instagram **@Cryst_alizedBoutique, @InnerPeaceHealings**

Facebook- **Deanne Millis- https://www.facebook.com/share/1ACuuvtzJR/ and Crystalizedboutique- https://www.facebook.com/share/19xnWYg35Y/**

Chapter Fourteen

By Tara Haley

Mum's The Word

Introduction

My name is Tara Leanne Haley. Through life's trials and tribulations, I have learnt not to judge a book by its cover. We each have a story to tell. Our journeys are all unique, our choices to make and our memories our to keep. All light casts a shadow …. I am blessed.

Revelations

As I lay awake at night thinking of years to come,

Scared I will be alone,

Alone without my mum.

As I lay awake at night thinking of what we have,

A tear rolls down my cheek,

I can't help but feel sad…….

The Journey

It was 1990 and I was 6 years old when my mum sat my brother and I down to tell us the news. My mum had a blood transfusion after a sterilisation and abortion went drastically wrong. The blood that the hospital had given her was contaminated. She had hepatitis C.

We did not understand the consequences and neither did my mum. You see she was not an educated woman; she couldn't read or write. Today it is recognised as dyslexia, but when my mum was a child, she was portrayed as a 'dunce'.

From that moment on, my brother, Danny and I lived in a constant state of fear. We believed it was only a matter of time before we woke to find our mum dead in bed. As time progressed, we noticed changes in our mum's behaviour. She would sleep all day and be awake all night. We would go to bed of an evening and wake up to a newly decorated living room or kitchen.

At the time we were too young to understand what this meant. It was a few years later that we started to realise what was happening. My mum had developed an addiction to amphetamine. We were led to believe that it was her medicine, the only thing that gave her the energy she needed to complete daily tasks. We would make her a cup of tea with a spoonful of sugar and a spoonful of speed. As children you do not question the actions of your parents, but as time progressed and our mum fell deeper and deeper into the depths of addiction, we had no choice but to question her motives.

Delusions

We would go to sleep of an evening and wake to a completely different home. Mum had been up all-night redecorating, walls would be knocked down, new furniture would be in place, it was like kaleidoscope of floral décor. We continued to take ourselves to school and do the things that children do. If we were sick at any point we learnt to write our own sick notes, Mums dyslexia was severe.

As Mum slept less and less, she started to develop paranoia, sleep deprived psychosis as described by my councillor or amphetamine psychosis. She believed that people were coming into the house through bricks in the wall. At one point she would lay there with a sawn-off shot gun ready to protect her property.

She would stab mattresses thinking people were hiding inside trying to rape her, although at this point strange occurrences had started to happen in the house, and my mum believed I was responsible for this. With hindsight I potentially did have some responsibility, at the time though I could not comprehend why my mum thought I was evil and had brought these spirits to rape her.

I was about 12 years old, and a group of friends and I had decided it would be fun to do a Ouija board. However, we got more than we bargained for! The board was highly active and said that we were communicating with a spirit of a friend who had not long passed away.

The details given by the spirit were perfectly accurate and led us to believe that we were in contact with the spirit that it had claimed to be. It told us of the cigarette brand that they smoked whilst living, the perfume it wore and a particularly important detail of how it had passed, which later was proven to be true after investigation by the police.

We used the Ouija board on a number of different occasions over the course of about 1 month. At times it would be incoherent and spell out ramblings, at other times it was clear and concise. On the last occasion we used it, the spirit we were communicating with told us that my mum would be back shortly, so it had to go. This was very unexpected as she was on a long journey, but the spirit said that there had been an incident on the motorway that meant she'd had to turn around. Low and behold, my mum pulled up outside within 5 minutes of us putting the Ouija board away, there had been an accident involving a lorry on the motorway.

It was not long after that the strange occurrences began happening. My mum claimed that she was being pinned to her bed of a nighttime by a malevolent spirit. She would go into a trance like state and begin automatically scribbling on a piece of paper. There was one occasion when she was thrown across the room in front of my brother and I by an invisible force.

We ran across the road to my nan's house who came over, and my mum was babbling incoherently. My nan proceeded to call a priest, who came and tied my mum to a chair with some old tights whilst standing over her with a bible all night reciting verses. It was terrifying. My Mum was adamant that I was responsible for letting these spirits into the house, and I now believe that I was. At the time all I believed was that I was an evil person and the world would be better off without me in it, and I started to self-harm.

It was around the same time as the Ouija board incident that a blonde-haired man knocked on the door one evening when my mum was at bingo. He said that his name was Edward Cartawick and that he had come to see my mum. I told him she was not home, but I would pass the message on. I remember thinking it peculiar at the time, my mum had a preference in men, she preferred tall dark and handsome, evident from the previous four marriages. On her return she explained that Edward was my biological father! I felt like my entire world had shifted on its axis...I was Tara Haley, daughter to John Haley. That night I lost my sense of identity.

Separation

In my mission to rediscover my identity, I rebelled. I questioned all that had ever come out of my mother's mouth, I could not determine fiction from fact, and I was consumed by darkness. I started staying out all night and drinking with older kids, I continued to self-harm, I became uncontrollable.

I still attended my appointments with my councillor, and I tried to explain why I felt the way I did. I told him of my mother's behaviour and the constant accusations and the extreme bouts of paranoia. It was at this point that my councillor reported my mum to social services, some people went to try to take her to the psychiatric unit but failed miserably.

This led to me being accused of trying to get my mum put away. I felt let down and deceived yet again by confiding in my councillor what was happening at home. It had led to more unrest, and I stopped attending my appointments. I became violent and would lash out. My mum had enough of my behaviours, she contacted the social services, and I was taken into their care.

I spent the next couple of years moving from house to house. I remember totalling 23 different homes during my secondary school years. I ran away from foster homes because they made me feel segregated from the rest of the family. I was placed with a variety of family members, friends' parents took me in, and I suffered sexual and domestic abuse.

Eventually my nan, my mum's mum took me in at the age of fifteen. She already had my brother living with her and my uncle in a 2-bedroom terraced house, so it was a tight squeeze. Living with my nan, uncle and brother was a whole new level of awareness, my uncle god rest his soul, was a troubled man, he was a heroin addict.

I recall returning home one day from being out with friends, I could hear my brother sobbing from his bedroom. I went to his bedroom door and nudged it open; it was dark, I turned the bedroom light on, within inches of my brother's hand was a hypodermic needle covered in blood. I literally saw red. I picked the needle up marched downstairs to my uncle, who was sat on the sofa, and threw it at him, like a dart, all the while screaming "if you are going to do these things at least have the decency to clean up after yourself!"

There were other instances when his heroin use caused issues. We would walk into him bending over the kitchen table whilst a friend would be injecting him in the bottom. He would miss his veins, and the area would swell like a balloon, and he would howl like a wounded animal. Most nights we would lay awake in bed listening to my nan and uncle arguing because he wanted money for his next fix, my nan always gave in.

One night I returned home with a friend unexpectedly, I was supposed to be sleeping at her house, but a situation had transpired that meant we had to change our plans. On entering my nans house, we were overwhelmed by the smell of gas. My nan sat on the sofa smoking a cigarette, I said, "nan it stinks of gas in here!" to which she replied, "I know, I've had enough." She had turned all the gas supplies on, the cooker, the hobs, the oven, and the gas fire, but not ignited them, she was trying to blow herself up.

It turned out she was going to be evicted from the property, she was giving all her money to my uncle and was in terrible arrears with the rent. I could not let this continue. I spoke to my mum about my concerns. I was just sixteen at the time and I thought if I got a job I could help pay the rent. My mum had a friend that worked in a brothel, she said "every woman is sat on a goldmine, if I had the guts I'd do it." I desperately wanted to help my nan, so at the age of sixteen I started working in a local brothel, I told my nan I was working at a casino.

I earned enough money to pay all my nans arears and get her out of debt extremely fast, whilst in that environment I felt separated from my own body, like I was watching someone else's life unfold. It was one day shift whilst I was busy designing posters for an event, we had planned that the owner of the brothel approached me, he sat down and asked me, "what are you doing here?" I explained why I had started working there, he was very open and honest and told me that I was better than this, I left the following week.

Path To Redemption

I got a full-time job working in a local service station, I finally felt like life was looking up. My best friend and I bought a house together and began our journey into adulthood. We were both young, only 18years old, and past trauma meant we found ways to avoid reality. Recreational use of drugs and alcohol became a problem, and we went our separate ways after 18 months of living together, although we remain friends to this day.

I had my first child at 21 years old, Malachi. It was at this point in my life that I started to realise the benefits of exercise for mental health and coping mechanisms. Although I had used it from being a child gymnast, joining the athletics team and football team at school, I was too young to understand the psychological benefits it provided.

I started yoga to help with the birth of my first child. Unfortunately, Malachi died in the womb at 30 weeks gestation. I gave birth to him on the 6th of May 2005. Within a year of Malachi's death, I gave birth to my rainbow baby, Tre and 5 years later his brother Kardell. Unbeknownst to me I had complex PTSD and in November 2015 I tried to take my own life. I swallowed 2 strips of amitriptyline with a bottle of vodka.

I woke the following morning. All the doors and windows in my house were open and I was laid in the middle of my living room floor. My nan came to see me and helped with the children so I could find my way out of the darkness. That is when the angels whispered in my ear.

Breaking Free

I moved 17 miles away from the toxic energy that had overwhelmed me. I took my two children to a beautiful village on the border to 3 counties. This was time for a fresh start. I started managing charities and helping the unemployed gain employment through coaching and interview preparation, I had a fantastic success rate. I had always had the ability to help others see their true worth through positive reinforcement and motivation.

I continued to utilise exercise as my own personal coping mechanism. Throughout the course of the past 8 years, I have gained qualifications online whilst working full time. I am building towards my ultimate destination which is to run a fitness and wellbeing retreat in the middle of the woods from a log cabin, accessible to all ages.

Resilience

Back in 2023, my nan started to get forgetful, it was Alzheimer's. I became her fulltime carer, whilst working fulltime and coaching strength and stamina to the young footballers and I burnt out. I was in the midst of an extremely narcissistic relationship and in May 2024 it all came to a head. I chose to leave fulltime employment to concentrate on my nan. My relationship came to an end and my mum was diagnosed with terminal cancer.

Nan's health deteriorated rapidly. One day she set herself on fire and if

I had not been there that day, you can only imagine what would have happened. I reported it to adult social care, and she was taken into fulltime care for her own safety. I transferred my caring duties over to my mum; we had a battle on our hands, my mum's cancer was a result of the contaminated blood.

Towards the end of last year, the Government had decided to take responsibility for all the contaminated blood cases. The EIBSS (England Infected Blood support Scheme) took over the caseload and after providing them with all the evidence and correspondence regarding my mum's medical history, she was awarded compensation.

My nan sadly passed away on 5th of November 2024 in the presence of my cousin, my eldest son and I, she went to the angels listening to her favourite Elvis song…suspicious minds. Mum has been given a longer prognosis than expected, the tumour is stable and localised, some good news amongst the chaos.

My mum's perception is one to be admired. She believes she would have died without the blood transfusion 30 years ago. Although she is going to die because of it, she has gained an extra 30 years of living. She has seen her children grow, her grandchildren and more recently her great grandchild, my eldest, he made me a grandmother at the age of 18 years old. She has been able to provide her children, my brothers and I with enough money to fulfil our dreams and buy a bungalow to live out her final days in peace. She will rest easy when the time does come knowing we are secure in her absence.

I continue my healing journey. I have regular counselling with an amazing therapist called Claire, I have used my money to set up a business so I can manage my time around my mum's care, and I practice self-care and gratitude daily.

After nan's death I chose to face my emotions instead of drowning them. I now lead a healthy balanced lifestyle; I practice what I preach and lead by example. I hope to inspire anyone I meet along this journey called life, especially the children I work with…because after all the children are our future.

Afterword

If I had been named after my biological father it would have been Tara Leanne Cartawick, my initials would have been TLC. That is where the name idea for my business originated, TLC Infinity. Over the past 8 years the initial business idea has evolved. I studied various alternative modalities during the evening whilst working fulltime managing charities.

I developed my portfolio with dedication and consistency and am now a qualified personal trainer, fitness coach, nutritionist, spiritual councillor, reiki master and crystal healer. I have practised yoga for 20 years, read tarot and continue to develop my skills coaching children's football strength and stamina. I am a firm believer that every day is a school day and to lead you must do so by example.

This year TLC Infinity became TLC Infinity Fitness, a combination of my cumulative skills. I now run a bespoke personal training business, helping others to achieve a healthy balanced mind, body and soul.

You can contact me at:

Facebook- **Tara Haley**

Facebook- **Tlc infinity**

Instagram- **tlc_infinity_fitness**

TikTok- **@tlcinfinityfitness**

Chapter Fifteen

By Karen Preston

I have decided to write about the struggles I previously had regarding mental health issues, from the dark depths of psychosis, fear of not being good enough, fear of ridicule, fear of others, fear of my surroundings, fear of speaking my truth, fear of love, you name it, I feared it.

I started with the belief that recovery is possible, started to challenge my limiting beliefs, self-healing, and working on self-love and have rediscovered myself. Complete transformation is possible. I am here to share my journey from broken to an empowered woman and finding out who I truly am along the way, and it is absolutely amazing!

Purpose

It was a beautiful spring morning in 2011. I was a passenger in a vehicle, returning home, admiring the view, and listening to music that had been recorded by my partner in a recording studio, a couple of weeks prior to this day.

I felt an urge to look up. I looked up at the windscreen; we were drifting to the other side of the road as my partner was becoming overtired. There was another car travelling on the opposite side, and we were veering towards it. I grabbed the steering wheel, pulling us back to safety again. This was so close to being a head on collision, until I looked up and took the wheel. The shock poured over me. I swore loudly, and the reality of what just nearly happened overwhelmed me with intense emotion. When I got home again, I sobbed.

I was in shock for days, even weeks, afterwards. I also felt so lucky that I was alive and went through thoughts of what would have happened if it wasn't a near miss. How would my daughter have coped? How would my family have coped? I also found gratitude in my life for being alive and having my loved ones around me. My emotions became fierce, and I wanted to give love to everyone in my life. I looked for ways to show this, as I was not confident in expressing my love for others.

I started to find joy in writing poems, journaling, and writing songs. I even discovered that I was not too bad at harmonising along with music using my voice. Shortly after that day in spring, I was down at a beautiful beach, just a few miles from my home. It was a beautiful morning. The sun was rising, and the birds were starting to sing their morning songs. On this morning, the sun looked somehow bigger and brighter than ever. It was huge, and it took my breath away. I had never seen the sun like this in my life.

It was the very first time I took in the magic of a sunrise and the way it made me feel. I was amazed at how incredible it was. I felt excited, and I also felt grateful for being able to witness this beautiful sunrise, the sunrise that stopped me in my tracks. I had witnessed a potentially life-threatening situation, and this made me realise how precious life really is and that is where I found the beauty in a sunrise and life itself.

When I got home, realisation hit that I now had a purpose; I just knew I was being guided. I remember saying aloud, "Oh my god, I have a purpose." I was unaware at that time, but my purpose was to guide and heal others. I was meant to be here for that.

Come To Me In The Light

I spent many months with my newfound hobby and would spend hours writing. It was around this time that I started to write about my feelings, the hurt that others had previously caused and even delved into the psychology of personality traits. I wanted to understand what made people tick. I had found my purpose but then doubts started to creep in. Earlier in the day, someone I trust had told me they believed I was being spied on. Here I was, with notebooks and sheets of paper strewn all over the table, whilst the darkness of the night crept in. I had been writing about events before this time, going into detail and with the most intense feelings. I was trying to release a lot of built-up sadness and anger. I was trying to make sense of it all. Suddenly, the information that I had been gathering about certain personalities made sense to me. The comment "They are spying on you," along with my thoughts racing and the information I had researched, had started to create a terrifying scenario.

Someone was at my window. I was in danger. I was being spied on. I could not move, and I found it hard to breathe. I heard noises; they were loud and like they were amplified in some way. The light of day could not come quick enough to light up the shadows in my garden and my home. I was frozen to the spot. I sat there for the whole night. This happened all the time I was in my house. I felt as if I was at the epicentre of some conspiracy. In fact, I was in the depths of a deep depression and psychosis. I never settled into my house after this.

Nights dragged on; they seemed to last forever, and the light of day could not come quick enough. I felt safe when daylight arrived. I was not sleeping at night, and this just fuelled the fears and heightened the hallucinations. I remember one night in 2012 when I lay in bed. I heard someone coming in through my front door and then heard them creeping up the stairs. I was about to be attacked, or worse, killed. The terror was real. I was sweating profusely as I was wrapped up in my duvet. Time was running out; I had to get help.

I called 999 on my mobile. I could not speak; the words never came out. Something made me hang up the call. It was now morning, and I was safe again. This is how I used to think; the dark was my enemy, as that is where the danger lurked. It lurked in the shadows, behind dark bushes, behind walls, and in my house. When the day arrived, that was my safety net. My safe place came to me in the light.

Shine Your Light

Many of my nights continued to be fearful and my days were not much better. I spent a lot of my time away from my house, away from the darkness as much as I could. I thought that this was never going to end, and my desires of healing and writing were only a passing fantasy. But things were about to take a different turn.

It was a Sunday in early December 2012, and I woke up realising I was pregnant. I knew as I opened my eyes, so I took a test I had in my drawer to confirm. My second child now existed, and I felt so much love already, just like my first. Later that day, as I and my partner got into our car, one of the songs he wrote and recorded a year previously began to play. It was called 'Shine Your Light.' I felt a rush of love and protection as I held my belly. We did not select this song, but it was playing at the perfect time.

This was now time for change, time to move house, time to be more stable for my eldest daughter and for this one too. I still felt uneasy in the house, especially on my own at night. This only spurred us on to move away from people from my past and to start our lives anew. My landlord agreed to end my tenancy in March 2013. We stayed with family until we were offered a house outside my hometown. I felt better as I wasn't living in the house that had all the memories of my turmoil. The fear left, I was sleeping properly, I was healing.

On her due date, July 24th, 2013, the church clock chimed as midnight arrived, and labour started. Everyone else in the house was asleep as

The Journey

I paced around, absorbing the contractions and breathing through them. I was going over the years that had passed, and I knew that this was about to be a new beginning for us all. I knew that everything was going to be fine. I knew I had to breathe through each contraction. 5.55am came and I knew it was time to get to the hospital.

It was a stormy Wednesday morning, and I even found my sense of humour during the drive. I said to my partner that I was thinking of the pain as "sand crashing on a wavy beach.". He was astonished that I was finding humour in this situation. Our daughter was born at 8.47am that morning, on her due date, and she was welcomed into my partner's arms, her Daddy's arms.

It dawned on me shortly afterwards that I had in fact seen all this playing out in front of my eyes a year before. Whilst sitting alone in my bedroom, I saw a vision of a baby being born. This wasn't a dream; I was wide awake, and it was like watching a film as I was looking at the wall in front of me and I saw my partner holding a baby. This vision was identical to everything, from the room to what my partner was wearing. It was incredibly emotional seeing a vision like that. It was a beautiful experience, but I did not share this with anyone else, up until this day as I had experienced hallucinations in the past and this would more than likely be misconstrued as just that, a hallucination. I had seen the day she was born, a year before it happened.

My partner and eldest daughter viewed our house later that day as planned, and we moved to a new town the following month. I loved where we moved to. I found a job in 2014, working as a carer and I loved it. As time went on, some of my previous fears would make an appearance. The hyper vigilance was back. I was contented living in our new town, and I was certain that something or someone would resent this, those who passed on that message 2 years prior.

During one of these episodes, I was sure there was someone in our garden. Any cars that parked next to the house were someone 'watching me.' This went on for a few years, and I thought at times that I would never get past it. Of course, these episodes meant I wasn't sleeping, and this made things worse. Although these episodes were rare, a lot less than before, the last time was late 2021 where I found myself in fear again, not sleeping, lack of trust towards others and feeling betrayed.

Promise Of A Girl

In October 2021, I left to stay with my youngest daughter for 3 weeks, where I found myself gradually finding my feet. Everything over the years had come to a head. There were things in my life I did not want, and I knew I had to leave, unsure for how long, but I knew it was right. After 3 weeks, I returned home and after heartfelt conversations with loved ones, decided that life was going to change. I had to change my mindset, to be honest with myself and find a way out of this spiral of darkness.

I worked on this from then on, gave up one of my jobs, even though I was worried about the decrease in wages, I wasn't truly living. Things were a lot better, yet I still felt anxious a lot of the time. I masked this with a smile and wine to finish my days. I felt like I was existing rather than living. By the end of 2023, I was drawn to a group on Facebook called The Soul Healing Academy. I had seen a post in the group about how much their lives transformed.

There are so many things on social media that promise this very thing. It is everywhere, and I had been curious about others in the past, but nothing sat well with me. Nothing drew me to look any further. So, I bypassed anything like this until I saw a post that was in The Soul Healing Academy with Gemma Elizabeth Williams. It grabbed my attention. I did not know this at the time, but I was looking for an "out" of how I was feeling and how I was living my life.

The Journey

Just before I saw this, I was feeling an overwhelming sense of sadness; I felt low; I felt unworthy, although I was living a good life. The post that caught my eye was something for members to do. It was a self-love exercise that entailed writing yourself a love letter. I was lacking self-love at this point in my life and most of my adult life, to be precise. I treated myself badly, although I was beginning to buy myself things that were beneficial to my health and my overall well-being. I was needing to act and become that 'better version of myself.'

Through my tears with a glimmer of hope, I searched for a leather-bound journal that was gifted to me 11 years prior to this day. I put my pen to paper and was writing my first words like this for the first time in years. I knew that I had to be honest with this piece of writing, a love letter to myself. Being honest was the hardest part in this. Earlier that day, I thought to myself, "I wonder if everyone would be better off without me?" I knew deep down in my heart that this was, in fact, a crucial part of turning this around. It was a crucial part of turning my life around after many years of self-hatred and self-sabotage. I released so much buried pain and anger. Things changed rapidly after this.

I joined Gemma's VIP Manifesting Academy the following month. Gemma has been running this amazing group for a few years, I had seen the posts on Facebook about it. One thing that Gemma said about joining this group is that it is the price of a takeaway a month. My higher self instantly said, well, I certainly had more than one takeaway every month.

My life shifted instantly. For the first time in my adult life, I had started to be honest with myself. Very quickly, I learnt that lies do not feel good; the truth does. Why was I putting myself down when I would not dream of doing that to anyone else? I now had access to many workshops that help with shifting a lack mindset into a growth mindset. I was drawn to a self-love meditation the same week I joined. I started to write each morning. I started to write what I was grateful for; this was anything from the sound of the rain outside to writing about what I would like to attract into my life.

I was learning about the Universal Laws, how to put them into practice, and how to raise my vibration, changing my life within weeks. Gone were the anxious ridden days, now I was waking up feeling grateful. I was relaxed, and I was on a completely different vibration. Practicing gratitude was a life changer. I was writing these down, the gratitude I had for the things already in my life and for the things I desired and wanted to attract into my life.

This is now standard practice for me. Each morning, I spend a bit of my time, which is not a great length of time, I may add, focusing on these things. People were asking what had changed as I was changing; my confidence was soaring in every aspect of my life, and I was starting to like who I was.

Here I am today, with no mental health issues or any sign of them. I am now embracing my spirituality by gaining healing modality qualifications, trusting myself and using the gifts I been blessed with. The murkiness of the psychosis and my gifts has now become clear. I know what wasn't real and know what is. I've not required a visit to any health professional or been medicated for years. Forgiveness has also played a part in my recovery. This was a big part of my healing process. Forgiving others and myself, moving on.

I made this written promise to everyone I love:
"I was sitting in the darkness, with the evening in my eyes.
You were lost in a world of nothing but the moon in the sky.
In your world with many colours, in a land with all your desires
I was sinking into the burning flames of someone else's fire.
Divinity now reveals me; I welcome you into my world.
Self-creation becomes your reality; I am your "Promise of A Girl."
You wakened me from my deep sleep; you opened my eyes.

The Journey

Begin to shine and radiate; will you let me be your desire?
Everyone looks to us and see what we have got.
It's something that everyone should have, but it can't be bought.
I could always feel your helplessness when you saw me close to them.
From looking straight into my eyes only sent you back into mayhem.
And as you look at me now, you will see it in my smile.
As a path of union and of service, co-create this reality; it's been worthwhile."

If you would like to connect with me, here is my Facebook account and group:

https://www.facebook.com/share/1AAqt9F1UG/?mibextid=wwXIfr

https://www.facebook.com/share/g/1C4tzomNQ5/?mibextid=wwXIfr

Chapter Sixteen

By Lynden Riley

"If you're gonna wipe us, we'll wipe you." And with these cutting words at my dying mother's side, it was the start of the end.

Spoilt Goods

Rewind to my younger days. I was born when my siblings were 15, 14 and 12. By the time I was making my way through primary school, they were just mere visitors in our house. Whilst it was similar to growing up as an only child, I was taught to share and share I did. We were poor, so there was never the opportunity to be the spoilt child. Yet, in my siblings' eyes they have always made it clear they believed that I was.

I always used to joke with mum and dad about how I was swapped at birth as I am nothing like my siblings. We are night and day with very little in common. My wanderlust to see the world and to be more authentic to who I am meant I was the child who pursued overseas travel. Following a desire to be more and do more, I moved halfway around the world to live. The others just didn't have the same drive as me. We were built differently, and to me, that's okay.

My move overseas trip prompted my mum to pluck up the courage to board a plane and visit. Together, we toured the UK and discovered what this country had to offer. Over the years, she came over again and again, and we managed to find new travel adventures. After almost 8 years living in the UK, I decided to move back home to Australia and brought a little cottage in the country with the folks moving around the corner. At this point Mum had experienced two heart attacks and dad was giving cancer a run for its money. So, I bought a block of land and built a beautiful big home with the idea of mum and dad living with me.

My father struggled to make the move, and I ended up alone in a gorgeous big house but not feeling settled. My siblings continued to show resentment towards me and all I achieved. Comments such as everything lands in my lap were frequent. What they didn't get, was I had inherited dad's work ethic, and I had worked seven days a week, saving, scrimping and barely having a life so that I could finally get what I thought I had desired.

I have never felt jealous of their lives, or dissed how they live, but they continued to have a bee in their bonnet about me. Our parents would always defend me when the backstabbing talk started when they came to see them. But to my siblings, that just meant the 'golden child' notion kept growing.

I moved back to the UK, selling up and knowing I would not be able to afford to come home. Although dad couldn't travel, mum came over to visit and we continued our adventures. My moves overseas allowed mum the opportunity to travel, something that I believe she secretly dreamed of since she was a child but never thought possible. Mum and I had many loves to share and had a strong relationship.

Back To The Future

Fast forward to Christmas 2023 and my usual Sunday call with my mum. She had been excited to be away from living with my sister and back in the countryside sharing Christmas with her old sewing group friends. She was happy and chatty as always except this time, she was sick. At first, she thought it was just the rich foods normally only consumed at Christmas. But after her stay with her friends, she just didn't go back to normal and she came home to my sister's house, where she was struggling to live with her.

"Guess where I am?" my mother asked, "maybe fluid on the lungs and we will know after a few tests." I had only spoken to her two days before when she called to wish me a happy birthday. "Back it up a little bit, Mum. What do you mean you're in hospital? What is going on and why hasn't anybody told me?"

There were a lot of thoughts running through my mind and the fact that no one had contacted me to let me know that my mum was sick really angered me. It turns out, that mum had been in hospital for a few days and was in such serious pain that they were running many tests on her. In the end, they had said they would make a decision on whether they would drain the lung and maybe that would work.

For some reason they also sent her home a few days after without draining her. On my daily calls to check in, she told me that she was back with my sister, and they'd already had yet another argument. Mum told me she wanted to sleep out in the garden in the cold because my sister was arguing that she shouldn't have come home. It wasn't mum's decision though; it was the hospitals. My mum was in so much pain that the following day they had taken her back again, and one more time I was calling the hospital.

You Decide

They drained her lung, and it was like instant relief. But then the bomb dropped. Mum said they thought that it might be lung cancer. I asked her if she wanted me to come home. "No, no need. They're telling me I have about a year to live and all I want to do is have my visit with you in May. They've told me that it should be fine, and I will be alright to travel to the UK."

The Journey

That's all she kept saying, she just wanted her trip out to me again in May. We'd already booked a lovely cottage up in the Lake District. Somewhere we hadn't been since the 90s. My mum was counting down for that trip, and it was all she was focused on. And while she focused on that, two of my siblings were focused on me and telling her that I was just trying to spend her money.

When mum first went into hospital and called me, I sent a text to my brother asking if he knew mum was in hospital. I got a short reply saying 'yes, but I'll know more once I speak to the doctor.' I then heard nothing. The following week when mum was back in again, I wrote to him and asked him what was going on. I wrote 'I spoke to mum yesterday; she wanted to sleep in the garden because she and sister had words.' The response was quite terse. 'It has nothing to do with her. The doctors believe that the cancer stems from when she had breast cancer which none of us knew she'd had.' 'Whoa, stop there', I replied. We did know she had it. She had it in the 90s and she had one of her breasts removed. We did know that because our sister was there. The next response was 'I'll know more when I speak to the doctor.' Again, silence.

I called and messaged mum every day to make sure she was okay. I said to her, "I don't know why they're not speaking to me. I don't know why my siblings aren't telling me what's going on." I also had texted mum stating that my siblings and I, we never speak, they never contact me, they never call me, and our only conversations are me sending them a text message to wish them a happy birthday. And you know, if they don't want to speak to me, that's okay because we don't have a relationship. It won't matter if they're no longer in my life. They're not there anyway!

I woke up early on a Saturday morning and found myself staring at repeated missed calls and messages from my niece saying that I urgently needed to call her. My heart sank. I had the message that they had moved mum to palliative care, and everybody had been told to come and say their goodbyes two days earlier. But nobody had told me. Nobody bothered. My niece thought that it was wrong and if it wasn't for her, I would not have known. I bolted into action and organised a flight back home to Australia. My niece got a video call to me so I could speak to mum and tell her that I was coming and to wait for me. Mum said, "don't worry it's OK" and I said "no, my tickets booked, I am on my way. You need to wait for me."

Showtime

When I walked into that room. My mum's face lit up. I will never forget that look. I got to say that I loved her and to share some more jokes with her over the next half hour. She closed her eyes, but she was still with us, still conscious. I thought that it was strange that my brother and sister weren't there when I arrived and then found that they had been but disappeared when I turned up.

Clearly something was going on there. They finally came into the room, and it was all very awkward with the hellos before quickly leaving. The next day, my sister turned up again. And in her usual way, started giving me a lecture. I asked why they hadn't bothered to let me know that mum had moved into palliative care and that they had been told to say goodbye.

She replied, "the hospital said you wouldn't make it." I replied "Bullshit! It's not the hospital's call." My sister continued mentioning that they did not have my phone number hence she wasn't able to call me. I called her out again. We have messenger. She could have sent me a message or called me on there. Then the truth came out. They had decided that I wouldn't have made it. "F*ck You." I screamed at her. "That's not your call. That's my call." Then she said, "And there's your attitude." We sat in silence for the next hour, me holding Mum's hand and wiping her face.

Then came my brother and his wife. We needed to move out of the room so that the nurses could clean mum and so outside into the courtyard we went. It felt it very strange when my sister and my brother's wife went back around behind me, and it just left me and my brother. Here we go. And that's when I got the 'if you gonna wipe us' conversation. It took me a moment to realise where they were coming from. Clearly, they had been reading Mum's phone and all our text messages over the years. I was disgusted. They had violated not only me but also our mother by reading her personal messages. Confronting my brother, I asked why he had not told me she was in palliative care. It was the same bs response that I'd had from my sister. "We didn't have your phone number." But you see, he'd replied to two messages on messenger. He could have made a call or sent a message, but he didn't.

"Let's have a conversation about being a family," I said. "I have friends that dropped everything in an instant to allow me to get on a plane and come over. My bosses had absolutely no issue. They just asked me to let them know how I was doing. My colleagues said to go, and they would pick up my work. They are my real family. But my siblings? Nothing."

My brother made a speech about how keeping in touch via social media is not really keeping in touch. We shuffled back into mum's bedside where I could once again hold her hand and continue to massage some oil into her rapidly drying skin. My mum's fingers wrapped around my hand just as much as my fingers wrapped around hers. She knew I was there. We held each other's hands my mum and me.

My brother's wife said to me, "you don't need to keep holding her hand, she doesn't know you're there." Before letting go of Mum's hand I told them that she'd been holding onto me since I arrived. Proving my point, I let go and, in an instant, my mum's fingers started twitching. The moment my hand touched hers, she stopped. She was still there. It was a relief when my brother and his wife left, and the unsuccessful ambush was over. But unfortunately, my sister stayed.

This is not how our parents brought us up. This is not how they'd want us to behave. I pushed my feelings aside and tried to make conversation. Finally, my sister went to sleep, and it was just me and mum. Her breathing was getting more laboured, and I knew it wouldn't be long. She opened her eyes and focused on me, and then a small tear formed. I told her it was okay. I told her I loved her and that everything would be alright. That it was her turn to be back with dad. I buzzed the nurse just as mum took her last breath.

The Beginning Of The End

The first thing my sister did was start throwing mum's stuff in the bin in the hospital ward. Her body was still warm. I had felt ambushed in the hospital and there was no way I was going to go back to my sisters to stay where I'd be in the middle of nowhere. It felt like there was more ambush to come. My brother was executor of my mums will. I heard nothing. Was she cremated? I heard nothing. Did they scatter her ashes as she requested with my dad's? I heard nothing.

It was then that I knew that it was all over. I don't have space in my heart, my soul, or my life for this negativity. I could not forgive and never will forgive them for not telling me about mum. It was not their choice to decide whether somebody could or could not make it. It was not right to read personal messages. It was not right to not let me know. The only thing I have of my mum is a necklace that she wore when she passed away. It has a little bit of my dad's ashes in it, and she adored it. My sister and my brother took everything. The only thing they could not take is my memories nor my love for my parents.

Managing my first Christmas without my mum has been hard. There was no card, no call. At this time of year there are constant messages, blogs and the stories about putting differences aside. Putting the olive branch out. It's time for family. Well, I'm here to tell you, family does not need to be blood relatives. It's okay not to put out the olive branch. It's okay to not want to talk to your family. And it's beyond okay to create a different family. A family of friends. A family who gets you, loves you, doesn't care what you have or don't have. They are the real family. The ones that are there when you need them.

Cutting The Ties

Having navigated that first Christmas and first birthday without mum and dad, knowing the anniversary of their deaths were rapidly approaching, it was time to cut the ties. My seldom media posting brother has posted videos that were clearly poised at me with my sister commenting. They were making their stance known loud and clear. I removed them from my social media and blocked them. I want no more from them but silence. My jokes as a child of being an orphan were coming to life, and I was at peace with that. What gave me strength was the new family I had around me and knowing nothing could take away what I had with my parents. I did a lot of soul searching, tribe finding, meditation and just talking to their photo. But it felt right. I had lived under the umbrella of sibling resentment too long. To those who write about putting differences aside as it's the 'right' thing to do and to those who start feeling pressure to reach out to family who they don't really care to – don't.

Society wants everything in a neat box with a pretty bow on it. Got to keep up appearances and look good to the outside. But if what's inside doesn't make your heart sing, then stop trying to make others happy. Don't be afraid to let go of what no longer serves you. In your life, friends do come and go, so can family. Trust yourself that you will be alright with your decision and don't care what others think about it. Find better things to fill your heart.

My journey into mindfulness began as a personal quest for serenity against the backdrop of family untying, and it has evolved into a professional mission to share these transformative benefits with others. I believe in the power of mindful living to change lives, reduce stress, and foster a deeper connection with the present moment. My serenity came after becoming a meditation teacher and now writing articles to give us all a little pep talk.

Let's connect and embark on this path to inner peace together at **www.strengthwithinunltd.com** and catch my regular articles at Lynden Riley on LinkedIn.

Life is way too short to not make my own happiness your first priority. It's not selfish, it's self-preserving!

Chapter Seveteen

By Charlene Cransten

My name is Charlene. I am a single mum of 2 beautiful children and my business centres on how I can help others that have been or are experiencing trauma like I have. I want to show people that there are alternative treatments that can help individuals from childhood and into their adult life. Reiki healing is a service that I offer that helps to reduce any type of stress or anxiety a person may be feeling. As a result, I have helped many people from all around the world who have seen the benefits from the distance and in person healing they have received. In the future I hope to continue this work and help as many people as possible.

Trauma And Me

It all began in 2010 when I had my second child, my son who is currently fourteen years old. As far as the pregnancy went, everything went very well. I had no problems during the birth and after eleven hours of labour my son was born weighing 7 pounds. It was scary when I became a single mother after having my first child, but the support I received from my family definitely made a difference.

I found the transition between one child and two children, as well as living on my own, to be very challenging at first. However, I eventually got used to it after the first few weeks, and I began to enjoy my new routine more. As opposed to my first child, when my second child was born, I noticed I was feeling down and depressed for the first time. Although I was not sure why, other people appeared to notice as well.

The Journey

The first time I experienced a trauma in my life was at that time. In contrast to the labour of my first child, which lasted two hours, the labour of my son lasted eleven hours, approximately nine hours longer than the labour of my first child. I was absolutely shocked at the length of my son's labour. Although I kept my house clean, I still didn't feel like myself even though the house was tidy. A visit to my General Practitioner led to my being finally diagnosed with postnatal depression in addition to anxiety, which I continue to experience even today. Despite being prescribed medication to control the symptoms, I found that the medication did not help me at all. I felt worse when I took it.

It was during a visit to Luton that I came across a stall in the market promoting the services of a holistic healer that I became interested in. As a result of this lady's invitation, I was able to experience this wonderful healing myself. The first time it happened to me, I thought it was only a massage, since I did not know what it was or what it entailed. In my attempts to relax, I fell asleep and within minutes I could feel my body releasing a great deal of stored trauma, feeling very cold for a few minutes and then feeling a wonderful sense of peace and calm for a few minutes after that.

In spite of feeling very low when I went there, I had an overwhelming feeling of happiness when I left. The first thought I had upon waking up was, "What did that lady do to me?" She told me that it was just universal life energy that had released all the negative patterns, unwanted thoughts, and trauma inside me, whilst replacing them with life force energy, leading to a more positive outlook on life.

The first step toward feeling great on the inside is to make sure that you are feeling great on the outside as well. I felt like I was winning the lottery after only one session, which was a great feeling. Although I was not emotionally attached to the place, I had to go back because the more sessions I had, the better I got. As a result, people noticed that I was thinking differently, and I had a different outlook on life. The biggest worry I used to have at that time was money and providing for my children's needs. I went for a number of healing sessions after discovering Reiki and went on to find out more about it.

Every time I went there, I became a better person as a result of my experience. It has helped me in all aspects, and it is something you can work on yourself if you are motivated. It has helped me for 13 years, and I still go for a top-up today because it has helped me in all aspects. It is my story that I am trying to share with others in order to inspire them. If you've tried massage and it helps, there are other avenues to explore.

I found that the more Reiki sessions I attended, the better, as it opened me up to new avenues for me that I was not expecting. In the end, I was inspired to learn Reiki, which seemed wonderful to me because I knew that it would benefit me in a number of ways. I wanted to share this with everyone, feeling empowered like Superman with his abilities. I wanted to heal everyone because there are so many old issues that can be addressed. There are many old souls and loneliness, and I want to share how Reiki has helped me. It can benefit many others, but there's a lack of understanding about it in this new age.

Inspired by my sessions, I found it as helpful as counselling, which improved my daily life with my kids, home, and family. Now, I have a better relationship with them and see things differently. This has led me to learn and teach Reiki and also Rahanni healing, which is a high level of healing—5-dimensional work with the higher Angels—that is absolutely beautiful. I also taught this, but the main point is how healing can help you. You don't have to be a single mum to receive healing; it's for everyone. There are many treatments, not just healing. If you need a massage to feel better, go for it. If you're feeling low, go for walks; it helps your well-being. Being outside is better than being indoors with a negative mindset. Being around positive people helps.

Cancer Survivor

In 2016, I was diagnosed with cervical cancer after experiencing abdominal bleeding. Despite numerous hospital visits and tests over three months, the cause was unclear. I was repeatedly sent home with medication and told it might be fibroids. Eventually, due to severe blood loss, I was admitted to the hospital for further investigation. I became stressed because I knew something was wrong with my body.

Long days and nights of uncertainty affected me in ways I still can't explain. I contacted them again and asked for help. They told me I'd have to wait months for a scan. I couldn't wait any longer. I asked what it would take to be admitted to the hospital. They said I'd have to faint first. I rushed to the A&E department, where doctors were unsure what to do. Eventually, a specialist admitted me for another night and scheduled a scan. The next morning, I had the scan and was told it could be fibroids.

I was discharged the following day, but fear still overwhelmed me. I couldn't go out or sit for long. The longer I sat, the more I bled. A week later, I had a minor operation to find out what was wrong. It was supposed to be day surgery, but due to blood loss, I had to stay. I went through a lot of emotions and was in and out of the hospital. There was no mention of cancer, and I was told I was too young for it. No tests were done. They kept saying it could be this or that. Just before they discharged me again, I had enough. I wanted to go home. My doctor said I didn't need a scan because it was just my period. But I fought all the way. We know our own bodies, right? Another doctor came just as they were about to operate. They came to my bedside with the results I was dreading, "Sorry to tell you this, but you have stage 2 cervical cancer." With my mum's support, I burst out crying. It was a shock to my system. I was so scared and had no symptoms apart from the bleeding. The cancer specialist gave me all the information I needed. Within a couple of weeks, I got the dreaded call from another consultant at another hospital. The emotions of not knowing and the what-ifs had a great impact on me. Off I went on the start of my journey.

After six weeks of intense chemotherapy, radiotherapy, and brachytherapy, I sat in the waiting room with my mum. My mind raced with anxiety, making me feel sick as the consultant called my name. In the room, we discussed what to expect and filled out many forms. I felt calm but also deeply scared, thinking only of my children and knowing I had to do this.

Start Of The Journey

As soon as I woke up on the first day of treatment, I felt sick and worried that it might not be as effective as I had hoped. In the hospital corridors as I walked through them, tears of peace came over me as I walked. As I sat in my own bubble during the first chemotherapy session, I listened to the stories of the other patients and talked with them about what I was experiencing. My perception of the process became more positive as I heard more about it, not only from the physical point of view, but also from an emotional and mental one. It was a pleasure to be treated by the doctors and hospital staff. Discussions about cancer were normal and inspiring, as a number of people were open about their experiences with the disease. There is nothing wrong with expressing your feelings, so don't be afraid to do so.

During the next five weeks, I continued the treatment. As a result of the side effects of chemotherapy and radiotherapy, I had some days where I wasn't well, but I also became mentally stronger as a result of those treatments. Additionally, I attended a few Reiki healing sessions, which helped me to process my experiences in a more effective manner. During these sessions, I felt a life force energy flowing through me, and I knew that the healing was helping me in some way.

As soon as I had finished my radiotherapy treatment, it was time for the last treatment, brachytherapy. This was the last treatment where I was required to stay for 3 days, eating and drinking were very difficult, and I had to lie in one position because of the radiotherapy treatment. A lovely lady offered foot reflexology. As a result of the radiation, there were no visitors allowed at the hospital, which made me feel alone. The surgeon told me that the operation and recovery process had gone well, and that the tumour had shrunk dramatically by the time I saw him on the last day. Having finally heard the good news, I was able to go home and to start living a normal life again.

I had to return for another consultation for the results. People came and went, and my initial thoughts flooded back. I was the last to be seen, and I went in filled with emotions. The consultant said I was free. I couldn't believe it and asked him to repeat it. The cancer was gone. I still had anxiety years later, fearing it might return. I couldn't thank the hospital enough for their care and positivity.

I'm glad I'm here as a survivor to tell my story, finally releasing the past I was holding on to. The support network of family and positive thinking helped me through this. I still lived a normal life while undergoing treatment—school runs, shopping, etc. I would rest when needed. It's a shame that Pap tests for ladies are offered at 25, which I believe should be lowered, and I will continue to fight for this.

Three years later, my mum started feeling unwell. Despite many tests, she was diagnosed with stage 4 lung cancer. I couldn't believe it was happening again to someone so close, especially after what I had just been through. My heart sank, and I broke down. My brother was with me, and I had to be strong and walk through those daunting doors again with my mum. Despite struggling with anxiety and emotions, my brother wasn't strong enough to do it. Her treatment lasted nearly two years with minimal side effects. She is a soldier, and I am thankful to still have her by my side as I write my chapter. The power of positive words and healing helps a lot with someone going through trauma. My daughter was young but understood enough. I now look back, close this chapter, and move forward, wanting to inspire others who have been through the same. Ladies, please go for your smear tests. It's uncomfortable but worth it. Luckily, I heard about Jade Goody, which inspired me to get mine done. It's a good thing too, as I wouldn't have known otherwise. No matter the trauma, you will get through it. There is always someone to listen and talk to; no one should ever go it alone.

Stay strong, there is always hope, and no one is ever alone. Connect with me on TikTok (Charlene22224) or Facebook (Charlene Cranston).

Chapter Eighteen

By Pixie Inanna

I am Pixie Nova Inanna, and my journey has been anything but ordinary. As a spiritual wellness coach and energy master teacher, I guide others toward alignment, balance, and empowerment. My path to this purpose has been carved from raw, lived experiences. Every lesson I share comes from a life that demanded resilience, transformation and belief in the divine spark within us all.

My story began with challenges that could have broken me. Then I became a teen mum, navigating the world while raising a child with little more than determination and hope. Those years taught me the art of resourcefulness, the depths of unconditional love. But life was not done testing me.

I am a survivor of sexual abuse and domestic violence, experiences that brought me to the edge of despair but ultimately ignited a fire within me. It was through these trails that I realised my strength, my worth, my calling. As I healed, I discovered the world of spirituality, energy work, holistic wellness, not just for myself, but because I knew others needed the guidance I never had. I learned to channel pain into purpose transforming trauma into wisdom.

I became a master teacher in energy healing, working with individuals to align their inner vibrations, clear emotional blocks, tap into their inner power and live more authentically. I don't just teach, I walk this path every day, embodying the principles I share.

I'm not here to play small, I don't believe in shrinking into boxes that society creates for us. I embrace my power, not only as a coach and teacher but as a Goddess – a woman who owns her divine essence and invites others to do the same. When you work with me, you're not just getting a coach, you're connecting with someone who has walked through the fire and emerged radiant. I understand the messy, chaotic and painful parts of life because I have been there. I know how it feels to lose your sense of self and how empowering it is to reclaim it.

I am here to remind you that no matter where you have been or what you have endured, you are capable of transformation. My work combines intuitive insight, energy alignment, and practical tools to help you rediscover your power, heal your wounds and step into the life you deserve. Your pain doesn't define you; it's the soil from which your strength grows.

Pad-Brat

As a child I was very different. I was blissfully unaware of how much so in my early years. Living on many army camps, moving almost every two years, with my mother and brother while my father was away a lot. My mother should and could have been a Seargeant in the army. Her organisational and leadership skills are immensely impressive all the more being that they come out of an elegant dainty lady. Skills which would be passed down to me but wrapped in a little hippie.

I was never taught about spiritual things, but magic and mystery seemed to always be around me. Whenever I shared my sighting of imaginary friends, fairies, flashes of colour around people, my dear mother would smile, listen and never ever told me I was being silly. I believe this to be how I've held onto such strong intuition throughout my life.

I was a lonely child despite the ever-growing imaginary friends. I know now these to be spirits who like my company. My brother was and still is my bestest friend. We had each other no matter where we moved, however uncertain things were, we knew that we were inseparable. Him being two and half years younger than me, he is the image of my mother and me in the face, but with the tightest ginger curls framing his ever-deepening dark brown eyes. By the time he was three people thought we were twins, due to him having dad's tall gene that I did not. It wasn't long before he surpassed me in height. He was and is my dear little big bro. His bond has saved me many more times than he even knows.

Attending several different primary schools in army camps was an adventure. I was not often accepted by the children in school due to my unusual ways. Trying out a new one always came with the nerve's and excited "is this the one I feel at home in?" I remember being six and telling children that I liked their colour… saying, "your light is really pretty" to a teacher and being laughed at by the other children. They did not ask what I meant. Even if they had, I could not have explained it to them then.

This only made school harder for me. My spirit friends would come to talk and play in school instead. I remember being so happy with them but this being when I knew they were different, I was different… and my little life started to become jaded by my gift. Conflicted with the love I felt, the magic I saw and the harsh reality that not all witnessed it. Which meant to me at that time I had to change to be accepted. So, I started to ponder the big things.

Why Am I Me?

Laying in the bathtub I took a big breath filling my little lungs deep with air, submerging myself under the water level. In my mind all I could hear repeating was the burning question "why am I me?" It just rolled around getting louder until I could not hold my breath any longer. As I opened my eyes ready to rise above the water, I was terrified by what I saw. I shot up taking the biggest gulp of air and was then paralysed into a sitting position almost touching noses with me! A full version of little six-year-old me just floating above! Smiling, looking at me so sweetly. She said nothing. Neither did I. But I felt a love like no other and a knowing that came over me that this was an answer to my question. And I was going to figure out what it meant.

I started to pick up on feelings that came with people's colours. Rather than bring up the colour I would ask why they were sad, mad or hurt? Some would just tell me, I guess not realising I had asked due to them needing a friend. Others would tell me shut up. Over the years I tweaked how I used what I felt, saw, knew and chose who to use my gifts with. Learning that I could change people's lights and colours with my loving words and by making them laugh.

Trails And Trauma

Navigating this gift alone in this way over the next few years brought many lessons. Some were comforting to my young, confused self while others were quite simply damaging. I trusted those that were hurt needed my help, my loving way. Not realising as a naive child that adults too can be so very cruel. My innocence was tainted far too young. That started the implode on my female energy and the decline in my self-worth. The confusion and numbness took over which made me keep my gift to myself. Not wanting anyone close, I turned away from it all, wishing it all to go away. I battled for it to go away for so very long.

I was always told I was pretty. Unfortunately, I experienced too many inappropriate actions from young boys after that first perverse experience. I became fearful of men, boys and being alone with them. As I got older and was able to control more of my own clothing and looks, much to my mother's disappointment, I chose to be more a tomboy as we called it then. Hiding my naturally slim and femininely shaped figure with big baggy T-shirts and skater style trousers. My long auburn hair always scrapped back in a basic ponytail and hidden under a cap. All in an attempt to appear less feminine, less pretty, less an object of desire, less a target.

I enjoyed skating and climbing trees, I genuinely did. I loved to draw scenes from nature on a soul charging sunny day. I loved to get lost in a fantasy tale, create and enjoy music, that little hippie was always in me and when I embraced those activities, I was completely at peace amongst it all. I was lucky to have a bunch of cousins nearby when we settled in South Wales by the time I was eight. I had my first experience of the big out and street life! Led by my cousin who owned her block back then. The roaming looking for friends, bobby knocking, hedge hopping, switching plant pots in people's gardens and causing innocent shenanigans were some of the best years of my childhood after so long on closed army camps.

I ended up going to a different secondary school than the friend group I was finally happy being a part of. This brought a new wave of loneliness and non-accepting relationships with the majority that I met through my preteen life. I lived for my weekend freedom with my group. Being so alone and feeling so unaccepted a lot of the time I started to yearn for love. By the time I was thirteen I had started to see more lights around people, no matter how hard I tried to shut it down again, ignore and deflect, it just kept on coming. Louder and stronger.

I noted the feelings I was getting when around people and started to silently psychoanalyse my information from the people I would encounter. I saw truths and evidence in the things I felt/ knew of a person that my gift had told me. I started to trust in my gift again. But for myself. I was not ready to share it again. I thought I could use it to my advantage. Build some information on these unusual humans... maybe this was my purpose- to collect intel on the normies?

Working through the minefield that was people I met a boy. A boy older than me. A boy who became the father to my older children. He accepted my weirdness, and he was my first love. Even though it was mixed up in a chaotic teenage love affair filled with clubs at a shockingly young age, sex, alcohol, drugs, lies to my parents, I felt loved then. To me it was love, attention, obsession, confusing declarations. How much I had to learn still about my self-worth then. I want to hug her so much when I think of those times. It was a raw rollercoaster which brought a love for rave music that still runs strong in my blood today.

My first son was born when I was fourteen. He was born in the May, and I turned fifteen in the August of that year. I was lucky to be supported by my parents to finish school. I remember my dear dad telling me that my life was not over… this is just a big hiccup that I know you can get over. My son was the catalyst for positive change. I knew I wanted him and that I wanted to be better for him. He ignited my heart and made my life and awareness different. And so started the fight to change my inner workings and break free. The next decade of my life I went through so many trials and transformations while bringing up children and desperately trying to hold onto a family unit. Without my dad and brother to tag in for the children I would be in a white coat rocking in a corner.

Studies, Single Parenthood And Self-employment

I had my own healing to tackle all whilst raising a little man. We had our own flat by time I was sixteen after some strained times in the family home. I decided to delve into spirituality in my own space. It became my sanctuary. I studied meditation and struggled to reach visuals for some time, concentrating on breathing techniques and colour work. I learned about chakras, energy, the universe and the powers we hold within. I found metaphysical studies fascinating, so many things made sense to me. This took me on a discovery of who I really was again after years of masking my true self. Being so isolated with my son was a gift from the universe. An opportunity to work on myself without distractions with a high vibrational focus of love for my child. My path was not consistent. It was messy and hard, dark at times. It was joyful at times too. It was empowering, progressive, it was change. Change is hard but so very worth it when you get there.

I had a profound meditation experience when I was around eighteen after practicing visuals and journeying, I had finally got there. I met my spirit animal first, a white wolf. Then I met my guide, Ezra. I had a special forest meditation space in my mind that I could visit them to gain insight and understanding which was so very comforting. I remember being so sad and angry about life's injustice so went into meditation to ask why I was having such troubles. I was dissatisfied with my guides telling me then that life was scripted to a point. I was handed a book and told, 'keep doing what you're doing. Your path will change dramatically at 33. 33?!' I was annoyed and confused at the time, and I had to process it and believe that it would. They had not steered me wrong since our connection started so I swallowed it, unwillingly for some time. Ezra started to speak and appear to me outside of meditation after this. I think she felt my distaste and need for extra guidance. I met more guides along the way who I work with regularly now. Each helping with different aspects of life and emotions.

I clawed for as much time as I could for my own growth, healing around being a single mum to three then four after two failed attempts at a family unit. I battled years of depression and hidden addictions. All in an attempt to cope and numb some of the big feelings. Once I learned that even though I was a high functioning addict, that those behaviours were hindering my healing and that feeling my way through was in fact the process I needed to face.

Through these years I found spirit and destiny magazine, and this is when I found Gemma Elizabeth Williams. I resonated with her in so many ways. Her energy and words spoke deeply to my soul, inspiring me to go for gold. I had wanted to become a version of myself I felt unobtainable until I heard her journey. A new fuel was thrown on my inner fire and it started to burn brighter than ever before. She was consistent and always authentically magical. A friend from afar before we even met.

I had struggled with failed relationships, romantic and friendships over the years. Each blow giving me a new direction and newfound faith in the universes plan. No matter how harsh, I would say, "everything happens for a reason, even if you don't know the reason yet!".

Brighter Future

My ability to continue to love myself, move forward, love on others and spread my knowledge to help others along their way, got me here today. My past and everything in it, the good, the bad, the ugly, the wins have all made me who I am today. The next part of my self-growth took me to study and qualify in areas that had helped me get through the years of soul searching and trauma releasing. I started to commit more time for my wellbeing. Growing my self-worth and really living and breathing all that was me. No matter who liked it or not.

I became a Master Reiki teacher. A metaphysical coach. Meditation facilitator and Sound Therapist. I have gained certification of many kinds in the holistic field including master herbalist, Yoni Goddess, Tantric Healing practitioner. Learning metaphysics, energy healing and meditation were pivotal to my inner healing and growth. Applying the principles raised my resilience to life's challenges and the personal mountains of trauma that crumbled inside me daily that kept me in a shell of a woman I was not happy in.

The Journey

Using spiritual practises, applying the principles I had learned to my daily life, along with the shadow work I had needed to face were the comprehensive toolkit I needed to repair myself. Slowly but surely, I have become more and more of my unapologetically authentic quirky self. I'm still levelling up. However, I face my inner self with more calm, acceptance, love and positive action now.

Releasing trauma around my feminine energy allowed me to step into my divine feminine power. This included deep inner child work. A tonne of shadow work, journaling, meditation and energy healing to compliment that. Accepting my feminine traits inside and out embracing their beauty, how ying and yang divine connections with the opposite sex can be, have allowed me to embody the woman I want to be. Knowing my worth and easily advocating for myself now. Leaving me feeling completely empowered as an independent fierce Goddess. Not allowing the past pain to dim my light any longer. Choosing to use my voice, experiences, embodiment of thriving to inspire and guide those who wish to transmute their trauma into passion and purpose.

So if you're ready to awaken your inner Goddess, embrace your energy, rewrite your story, I'm here for you. Together we will turn challenges into triumph and create a life that feels aligned, abundant and uniquely yours.

Let's rise, reclaim and shine in your power!

You can find me at:

Instagram- **Pixie Inanna**

Facebook- **Rainbow Pixie**

Email- **PixieInanna8888@gmail.com**

Chapter Nineteen

By Shelley Fifer Richardson

Second First Chances

Hi, I am Shelley, and I am the founder of The Snoring Squirrel Wellbeing. At the time of writing, I am 44 years young and will forever be in this book! Hooray! Snoring Squirrel is a mixture of holistic therapies including Usui reiki and guided meditation groups. These are especially good for those experiencing burnout, or peri menopause/ menopause. I also practice Eft (emotional freedom technique or "tapping") chakra healings, and oracle cards readings.

Ever since I was little, I knew there was magic in nature, the moon, energies and spirits. I even believed I could talk to animals... maybe I can. I had a little altar with candles, shells, sea glass and of course crystals. But, like a lot of things back then in the 90s, it wasn't really the "done thing" so it all got packed away. I got a "real job" after college and proceeded onwards. A part of me felt like it was missing.

Throughout my 20s and into my 30s I just stuck to admin/medicals roles simply because I could do them. Looking back, I wish I had pursued working in marine biology or in wildlife photography. While I was always confident externally, at times internally could be quite different. My natural spark had to be dimmed as I was told I was "too much" "too happy" "too positive." Many people came and went in my life. I didn't realise how much I had allowed some people to take advantage of me for the sake of feeling needed, wanted or good enough. Losing my dad at 28 was a big blow, and a part of me died too and never came back. You don't expect to lose a parent in your 20s, if indeed ever!

In 2017 I had major abdominal surgery, and a huge fibroid was removed (the size of a grapefruit) from the wall of my womb. At 35 I was told I would need a hysterectomy, but thankfully a wonderful surgeon took me on and performed the surgery as he knew I wanted children. I couldn't walk well or do much for weeks on end afterwards. It was during this time I realised things in my life, particularly my job wasn't healthy for me. But fear of change kept me where I was.

Fast forward to 2019 and while struggling with a toxic environment and losing 2 pregnancies, I reached out to Gemma who runs the The VIP Manifesting Academy (manifesting, soul sisters) and finally found I had come home. I learnt lots about myself, how I was stopping myself from being happy. It was also where I learnt to become a practitioner in her accredited courses from Silver Violet flame to Reiki.

What Is Happening With The World?

When lock down hit, I was pregnant with my son, I left work for what I thought was going to be a few weeks, to not being able to see anyone for months on end. It was such a stressful time. Hospitals wouldn't allow my husband in for scans, so we had to pay for a private one. I was very sick with hyperemesis gravidarum, stuck in a one-bedroom flat with no garden, and only allowed out for an hour a day. My mental health took a toll, as I felt distraught, I couldn't enjoy my pregnancy or being with my loved ones. At least living in the countryside, it felt "safer" than other places in the country. After giving birth, it was months before people met him. Thankfully a lovely lady kept running a singing group for young mums (outside) so I did manage to make some new friends. But maternity leave wasn't what I had envisioned!

THE JOURNEY
Things Can Change In A Heartbeat

I had struggled to conceive my son, so in 2022 while enjoying a break away in the sun, I happily discovered I was pregnant again. We all had a sickness bug prior to going so when this continued, I just assumed I was taking longer to get over it. My son was turning 2, so it was perfect timing. My egg count was very low, and I was due to go to the clinic when returning home. I remember calling them to tell them my news, they were delighted for me.

Two weeks before the holiday I had found a lump in my breast. I had been going to the gym for months and my personal trainer was putting me on machines that had hurt my boobs. I previously had cysts before so wasn't concerned. The doctor referred me straight away but without much fuss. When finding out I was pregnant, I thought it might be due to that. A painful breast isn't normally listed as a concern (except from Coppafeel) so I had my ultrasound and biopsy without a care in the world.

That Room

After a big 2nd birthday party for my son, I was called back to the hospital and told to bring someone. This made me nervous but again not too much. The doctors came out, smiled said hello, but the look they gave me made me hold my breath. I said, "I assume all's okay?" They replied, "no it's not, it's cancer." There was a pause, then I said very calmly, "I'm pregnant." I don't know who was more shocked, them, me or my mum who was with me. I expected to cry but I went into autopilot firing questions off at them, gathering all their booklets and swept out of the room. They agreed to scan me weekly before making a plan of action.

Shit Got Real

My diagnosis was Grade 3 IDC DCIS oestrogen positive breast cancer. While trying to navigate the fact my body was trying to kill me, my morning sickness was ramping right up. Because I had suffered from HG previously, and this was going the same way, I thought everything was well. I'll never forget the faces of those 2 nurses while on that last scan day, utterly sympathetic about my diagnosis, but then the monitor showed no heartbeat, we were all lost for words. I was distraught. How could my body still be making me so sick when she had gone?

Sadly, this wasn't the end to the heartbreak, I had to be scheduled for assisted surgery to then be able to start my scheduled treatment. I was made to feel like a wanton hussy by the surgeon and offered the coil to "stop this happening again." I broke down as I screamed at him. I had cancer, lost my precious baby, but she hadn't left my body yet. To this day I regret not making a formal complaint about that surgeon.

The Big Bold And Ugly

Nothing quite prepares you for Cancer. You see it on Facebook, the news, family or friends possibly, but when it's you, it's surreal. My surgery, a therapeutic mammoplasty (both breasts cavities/lumpectomy and some lymph nodes removed) was completed by December 22. Christmas was very strange. I felt like I was half in and half out. Lots of pain and not being able to pick my son up or have our big cuddles like before. We had to invent games. Piling up cushions over me so he could climb up over 'mummy mountain.' And later on, during chemo, who can crawl up the stairs or scoot down on their bottom first.

It's not an exaggeration when I say that during chemotherapy, it was the closet I felt to death. This is NOT me trying to put people off or tell you not to do it. Everyone is different and reacts differently, but for me it was hell. I had a hickman line inserted into my chest, rather than arm as I really thought I'd still be able to work and also be able to still carry my son. Financially I needed to continue to work (having already been off work for weeks after surgery), but after my second round of chemo, and being told off by my district nurses, I had to stop. When you're torn between money coming in but also your health it's gut wrenching. There is limited benefit support for cancer patients, this needs sorting asap, as well as the quickness of decisions.

My first round of chemotherapy was in February 2023, I barely made it home and up the stairs, as family looked on. My aunty Helen took me to each round, and home again. I barely said hello to my husband or mum, my son calling for me as I crawled up the stairs feeling weak and dizzy. I could see they were visibly upset that they couldn't do a thing for me. All night I was so scared, heart palpations, hot flushes and pain…then came the sickness, legs like jelly trying to stand up, and quietly trying to vomit so not to wake my son.

Even though I had cut my hair short, when I ran my fingers through after my first round, some clumps came out, it was devastating. WORSE was that I even felt angry at myself for being upset. I had cut my hair short hadn't I, I was in control, wasn't I? But control is the illusion.

You read all about hair loss, but it doesn't prepare you. I thought I was prepared, had long hair cut shorter and shorter then shaved off completely as all the clumps made me look like I was dying. Seriously I looked like a mummified skeleton. My son was so scared of me when I walked in, it broke my heart, but once he touched my bald head, he couldn't stop giggling. Losing my eyelashes and eyebrows where the worst. I couldn't wear my eye makeup, which made me feel more like me. I felt like cancer had completely stripped my identity away. You can cover your head with a wig or scarf, not your face. Steroids made my face puffy and red, like a jelly baby.

People would see me out, and some would just cross the road, like I didn't exist, or they could catch cancer. The district nurses came weekly to flush my line. They were my lifeline, my confidants and just amazing really. During the days where I could barely get out of bed, dressing myself was so painful, even just breathing at times. I had some solace in my son's bouncing energy, but also my beloved dog Ernie. (At the time of writing this, he has sadly passed over the rainbow bridge. I am utterly heart broken and feeling so lonely without my little shadow. The stairs were hard for him, but he still made it up to me making sure I was alright. I swear he could smell the chemo and would squeeze so tightly next to me). Being stuck inside with no energy to do anything is isolating and suffocating. I resented my husband being able to get up and go to work, even though he has MS, while I was stuck on the sofa for hours on end. Ernie wouldn't leave me though; I have no idea how I would have coped otherwise.

What Fresh Hell Is This?

Chemotherapy and radiotherapy can affect people differently. Sometimes I had to suck pineapple to get rid of the metallic taste just so I could drink water. Not using metal cutlery as well. Pure aloe vera gel on radiotherapy burns is a game changer. Particularly if you apply straight after treatment but remember do other side i.e. your back as it enters and exits your body. My GP was great, giving me tablets to soften poo and other gel to wash my mouth with to soothe the ulcers.

So, if your GP doesn't know much about cancer, ask for someone who does. Little Lifts charity sent me a chemo box. It was full of really useful things from chilli oil, tea bags, eye masks etc. You can also order one for free to send to someone. Eat and drink what you can. They bang on about only healthy food to get you through, but some days that might have to be bags of crisps and chocolates. 3am seems to be the scariest time to be awake, you feel all alone in the world. But any issues I knew I could always ring the ward nurses. I was still very lonely. Just as I was finishing treatments, my appendix flared so I had to have emergency surgery. They found another primary rare cancer but thankfully it hadn't attached!

The NHS provides wigs for you, each trust is different, some give you them for free, others you have to pay. The choice I was offered (that I had to pay for) made me look like an extra from any popular 80s shows. I tried to make light of it and posted some pics on Facebook. Gemma (VIP Manifesting Academy) and my gorgeous soul sisters clubbed together to buy me a real hair wig. I can't tell you how much that meant to me or how much it helped on days I wanted to give up or just look like me again.

I Just Can't Mum

The hardest thing about all of this was and still is, not being able to be the type of mum I wanted to be for my son. Crawling on hands and knees, not being able to lift him, relying on people to be with me just to walk up into town with him. I will be eternally grateful to my family and friends, especially my mum, Claire, Amy, Dr Yvonne aka the oracle, to name a few who helped me so much. But at times I just wanted to scream, "leave me alone! I can do this," (I couldn't) but relying on people wasn't in my nature. I was the one who helped people. I was also so frustrated with myself, then at family, then mum guilt, then back at me. Vicious circle!! You feel trapped, lonely, scared, and angry all in the space of 5 minutes.

I hadn't allowed myself to grieve my loss, I had to just focus on getting through each round and on my son. But knowing I'd never have any more children broke me. I truly believe though she had come to save me and wasn't supposed to stay. One of the hardest things now I have my hair back and look relatively normal, is people saying, "Oh you look so well, you're over the worst now" (meaning finishing chemotherapy). Please don't say this to someone, I know you mean well. I'm still dealing with lots side effects, be it from monthly implants keeping me in a medical menopause, daily tablets and 6 monthly bone infusions.....sometimes I think it's worse than going through chemo!

I now try and help other people I meet at the local cancer support charity in my town. I am lucky all my family and friends still help now! Weekly acupuncture has become a lifeline, without it I truly struggle. So, I would recommend it to anyone, cancer or not.

Becoming Snoring Squirrel

I had already learnt some healing modalities, but this amplified during my treatment. I found having Reiki or EFT sessions really helped get me through a lot. The red squirrel fascinated me, it manages to still hold on against the grey squirrel but both species hibernate in winter. That spoke to me. I saw myself as a squirrel going through hibernation and waiting for my spring! So, it became my logo, with the help of my sister's talents.

My mission is to become a multi qualified wellbeing practitioner with the view of helping others, especially in the same situation as me. Modern medicine is wonderful but there is still a place for holistic therapies. Reiki and massage are offered in local force centres.

I came up with my guided meditation circles to focus on women going through menopause or experiencing burnout. What I found helped me I could share with them. Thankfully speaking about things now isn't such a taboo subject, and we must start putting our needs first. If it wasn't for cancer, I wouldn't be on this path now to help others. But also, to help myself live my second chance at life!

The Journey

We are at the end of my story, I hope there are some things that might be of use to you. I'll leave you with this quote from Tim Ferris that really spoke to me.

The question you should be asking isn't 'What do I want?' or 'What are my goals?' But 'What would excite me?'

If you wish to connect with me, I'd love to hear from you. You can do this by emailing me on:
Thesnoringsquirrelwellbeing@gmail.com

Alternatively, you can follow me at:

Business page: **The Snoring Squirrel Wellbeing https://www.facebook.com/share/1QA4Kj56hJ/**

Instagram **https://www.instagram.com/thesnoringsquirrelwellbeing?igsh=bDE5YXQ4NWU1OTFv**

Facebook: **TheSnoringsquirrelwellbeing private group for members.**

Chapter Twenty

By Lorna Hammond

Journey To Spiritual Expansion

The Beginning

My mum was nineteen when she became pregnant with me. My mum and dad stayed with my Gran and Grandad until they got a house. I loved the house I grew up in. It was a two bedroomed terraced house in a council estate. There was a cul-de-sac at the back. Nobody had much but we all shared. I remember having to go to my neighbours for milk or sugar on days we ran out but had no money. Can you imagine if I did that now? All the families struggled but we all helped one another out. My dad was a builder, and my mum worked at the local factory. I had a lovely childhood playing on my bike, making up games, playing outside until my mum called me in. I was an only child until age 8 when my brother was born. I was a very shy child. I was bullied all through school due to being quiet.

When I was twelve my mum had enough of my dad going out drinking and not coming home, she packed two black bags full of clothes and left. We moved in with my gran and grandad. The three off us in their spare room. I slept on a camp bed which was like a sun lounger and many a morning I would wake up with my legs in the air and my head on the ground as the legs collapsed. I blame that for the reason I am so clumsy now, I spent too much time with my head upside down!

Mother Wound

After a year, my mum got a flat in one of the worst streets in town. There was never a dull moment. I left school at 15 to be a hairdresser but that did not last long again, the bitching and egos was not for me. When I was seventeen, I went to college and my mum had started seeing a guy 11 years younger than her. He was a drinker and would come in drunk smashing up the flat and abusing my mum. One night I had enough, and I went through and confronted him. He went to hit me, I remember it like it was yesterday, his face went pure white, his eyes full of rage, he lifted his arm up to hit me. I was terrified, I started hyperventilating, I could not get a breath. My mum managed to intervene and calm me down. She said she would take him to his house and finish with him in the morning when he was sober.

I was so relieved and happy to get rid of this monster or so I thought. The next day I looked out the window and saw them walking up the street hand in hand. I was devastated and so angry I packed a bag and went to my mum's friend's house. She telephoned my grandad, and he came to get me and I stayed with them until I bought my own house. It was the first time in my life that I felt safe. I could sleep at night without worrying if I were going to be woken up with arguing and the flat getting smashed up. My mum is my best friend now and I cannot imagine life without her she helps me so much (she is no longer with him thankfully).

Feeling Free

I spent my teenage years supporting the Fife Flyers, the local ice-hockey team, and the ice rink was also my safe place. I loved ice skating and going to ice hockey matches. When I turned eighteen, I started going out clubbing. I loved it, alcohol gave me so much confidence and the dance floor made me feel free. When I was twenty-four, I met my husband Stephen at the local gym. We moved in together and we got married in a local castle where I felt like a princess. We went on to have two beautiful kids.

The Day That Changed My Life Forever

My husband and I went on holiday to Amsterdam with another couple. We went to the coffee shops for edible cakes. It was not my thing at all, but I just went with the flow. The first shop we went into, it was a laugh, we were hysterical, but we had to take it further and go in another shop. Little did I know that moment of stupidity would change my life forever. I started to feel so unwell; the hotel walls were coming in to me, I had never felt so bad. I asked Stephen if we could go out for a walk. We walked for miles, and I was hoping to walk the feeling off, but it did not happen. We decided to go back to the hotel and try and sleep it off. I remember getting up at 5am and still feeling high. I thought I was never going to feel 'normal' again. I went back to sleep and when I woke up, I finally felt like myself again. One week after we got home, I had my first ever panic attack. I thought I was going to die. I became obsessed thinking I was going to stop breathing. I was off work for months, I never wanted to be alone in case I died. When Stephen went to work, I would go to my gran's. I was so bad I had a community psychiatric nurse that I saw weekly for about a year. I have battled with anxiety every waking day since then until recently (more on that later).

The Day I First Realised There Was More To Life

My first experience of death was watching my Grandad who I lived with and was like a dad to me get a diagnosis of stomach cancer. I watched a big strong man deteriorate. He ended up in a hospice. I remember we went to visit him one night and the nurses told us to stay as he did not have long. My mum and gran nipped away for a coffee after being up all night and I sat with him. I remember begging him, "Just go, please I will look after Granny Etta". He died an hour later. I went to visit him in the funeral parlour and it was so surreal, it did not look like him at all. I was not spiritual then; I grew up being told, when your dead your dead that is it, but something hit me that day. I knew that his physical body was separate from his soul. I just knew he was still alive, and his physical body was the shell that carried your soul. This was also confirmed to me when my Gran died. Granny Etta was like a second mum to me. I lived with her until I got my own house, and she helped me with my anxiety. She made me feel safe. When she was dying, she was shouting out for her mum. I knew my great gran had come to meet her when she passed over.

Father Wound

Before my mum and dad split up, my dad was hard on me. He tried so hard to toughen me up. When my mum and dad split up my dad met Joan. I never got to visit their house, in fact I only saw my dad on birthdays and Christmases. Once, I got my own house, he started visiting every Monday evening by himself; Joan did not want anything to do with me. He was the best grandad to my two kids Olivia and Noah and my brothers three kids.

One day when he visited, he told me he had been coughing up blood. It was confirmed a few weeks later that he had lung cancer. My dad had been working in buildings with asbestos and developed asbestosis. My dad was so brave during his cancer journey. He got one of his lungs removed, this was when I spent more time with my dad. We would go out for drives in the car, and we would chat and laugh. I really enjoyed getting that time to spend with him, I am forever grateful.

This is when I started to see more of my step mum Joan, we were civil or so I thought. I found out later that she was making up stories about me and telling people things that were not true (I did not find this out until after my dad died). On one of our drives, he told me about wanting to write a will, but Joan would not allow it. He asked if when he was about to die could he give me his bank card to their joint account and withdraw a generous sum of money. I told him it does not work like that; the bank would need his permission. We talked about Joan and how she would not let him write a will and about death. He said, "you will not want to be there when I die?" I told him "I would", he said "I don't understand that, why would you? Why do people want to watch you die?"

He also told me that Joan would not cope once he died and warned me, "if she starts, please wait until I am in the ground". I knew things would change between me and Joan when my dad died, I just had not prepared myself for how bad and fast it would be. When we got the news about my dad, we told the kids that grandad was extremely ill. Noah who is now diagnosed with autism said, "Grandad's going to die on his birthday". Now this was in December and Noah had no concept of months/time. At the time I never thought that much of it, but it did stay with me and the family.

My dad was struggling to swallow food. This is when we found out the cancer was back. He was admitted to hospital and told he had months to live. I just knew it would not be that long. My step mum would go to hospital and sit all day, she would not let anyone be alone with my dad. He desperately wanted to make a will, but Joan would not let him.

My dad got discharged from hospital on the Friday. When I went to see him on Tuesday morning it was his 62nd birthday. He was sitting up with his clothes on, but he was shaking and sweating. I took one look at him and started to cry. We hugged, that hug meant so much to me, we never cuddled or said I love you. He got up and went over to the bed that was set up in the living room and fell asleep.

The Journey

Joan needed things from the shop, so I nipped out. I told my dad that I was nipping to the shops and would be back. He said 'ok'. When I came back my dad was unconscious. I knew then he was going to die, I went into a panic and told Joan I was nipping home to give the kids lunch and I would be back. I telephoned my brother Colin who was at work. I told him to leave work as I did not think dad had long. He rushed to see him. I had lunch and was about to head back. I telephoned Colin; the doctor had just been and had given my dad an injection to help him along. I jumped into the car and drove to my dad's and just as I arrived the telephone rang. It was Colin telling me that dad had died. He said, "Where are you" I said, "I'm outside". At first, I was so angry with myself for leaving then I spoke to a friend who told me he chose to go then, then I remembered he did not want me to see him die.

Everything was fine at this point and Joan asked us both to help arrange the funeral, we met the celebrant and funeral directors. My dad was at the funeral parlour, and I could not decide if I wanted to go or not. One morning I got up and thought 'I will phone and see if I can go now.' I just needed to do it then whilst I felt brave enough. My mum was here, and I asked her if she could come with me. She came in with me for a second then waited in the waiting room whilst I stayed with my dad. Little did I know what was about to happen next.

Joan telephoned me that night and she had been asking the parlour who had been in. She was furious that I had taken my mum for support. I begged her not to start but she slammed the phone down. I never heard from her again. We telephoned her and messaged her and even contacted her sister but nothing.

Colin went along to see her before the funeral to find out what was happening after she gave him the details and she started on him. The funeral was awful. It did not feel like my dad's funeral; Joan's name was mentioned more than his. She did not attend the tea after the

The Journey

funeral she just went home. We tried to contact her, but she just ignored us. We had no idea what was going on with his ashes. We thought he was going in the cemetery as that was initially said, but I don't think he is there.

For years Colin and I struggled, we tried to take it to court but we both got so unwell with the stress we just dropped it. We were not interested in the money it was the principle. We have no idea where my dad's ashes are, we have nothing sentimental, it broke us. We bought a bench in his memory, so we had somewhere to go but it still did not feel right. I became fixated with his ashes and where my dad was. This continued for years, making myself ill. During my grieving I started to write poems it really helped me express what was going on in my head.

Here is one, I swear I can write a book of grief poems that I wrote during this time.

Dad

I don't know where to put this.
As we have no place to go.
Your wife has been so selfish.
How she sleeps at night – I do not know.

I have reflected on the past a lot.
She has had this all planned.
She always knew that she would keep you far away from us dad.

You told me this would happen.
How you stayed with her, I do not know.
She never accepted your family.
from day one, it was all a show.

The kids are missing you greatly.
They do not understand.
We all just want a place to visit.
To be near our dad and grandad.

We have nothing sentimental.
It makes us all so sad.
To not even know where your ashes are.
How can anyone be so bad.

I know you will be so proud of us.
Your family have been too.
We have been to hell and back.
Loving you has got us through.

You are in our blood; she can't take that.
Or our memories too
How she denied your dying wish
Did she ever truly love you?

We think of you every day.
You're always on our minds.
We just hope that you are at peace now.
And it will get easier for us in time!

Spirituality- My Awakening

My first experience of spirituality was when I trained to become a Reiki Master. I then trained to become a Belief Coding® Facilitator. I was crippled with IBS and anxiety and after 2 sessions my social anxiety was so much better that I was able to go to see Harry Styles in concert. I have helped so many people including myself get rid of their subconscious beliefs and reframe them into positive ones. Belief

Coding® also helped with not feeling good enough, low self-esteem, and feelings of abandonment from both parents growing up. It also gave me the confidence to start my own business.

I started to become more spiritual at this point and decided to have a Going Beyond the Veil session. The first person to come through was my dad, (this was 7 years after he died). I was able to get closure, after all those years. My dad is one of my spirit guides. I no longer feel guilty or unwell as my dad is here with me every day. I got so hung up on his physical ashes when his spirit is guiding me every day. I am now a practicing Psychic Medium, Activator, Belief Coding® Facilitator, Spiritual Coach and Going Beyond the Veil Facilitator. I love taking people beyond the veil to meet crossed over loved ones and help them get the closure that they need to move forward in this physical world. I also have been activated with light language (the language of my soul) and incorporate this into my healings.

I just want people to know that ANYBODY can connect to their spirit guides and receive guidance. I was not born with the gift. Awakening was the best thing that happened to me. I have made so many like-minded friends, I have a full heart every day helping others and I feel so aligned. I am now grateful for the lessons Joan taught me. I know I had to go through all these challenges to be who I am today. A Lightworker/Healer/Coach/Activator bridging the gap between worlds, spreading love and light to everyone I meet and helping them heal, activate, and ascend living a soul aligned life.

If you would like to connect with me my free Facebook group is Awaken and Transform with Lorna.
https://www.facebook.com/groups/2569790203191789/

Reiki Master

Belief Coding® Facilitator

Going Beyond the Veil Facilitator

Spiritual Coach

Psychic Medium & Light Language Activator/Healer

Chapter Twenty-one

By Leigh Stierle

The Beginning

When I was a little girl, I was a Daddy's girl. I always wanted to be with him or near him. I was 7 years old when my older sister and I watched him get on a plane. With tears streaming down my face, I knew he was not coming back. He did not come back, and I fought to see him again until I was 16 years old.

Dealing with those fears of abandonment with him leaving has made it more difficult to get close in romantic relationships. A few years after he left, my mother started dating again. We moved in with my stepfather and he started molesting me at 10 years old. It lasted for a year. Of course, he treated me poorly and it wasn't easy growing up in this household. I did not tell anyone and to this day my mother doesn't know. I know she would find a way to make it my fault. I had a very verbally abusive stepfather, an older sister who is an alcoholic whom I no longer speak to and a cold and distant mother.

As a kid growing up there were no hugs or anyone saying, "I love you." Growing up I had a great group of girlfriends who really were like family. We did everything together; I had met them all in the 5th grade. We would go to the movies and school dances. At high school it was dating and beach parties. With having the abandonment issues and what my stepfather did it's very difficult for me to have romantic relationships. I don't know what it's like to have a healthy love. Well, the healthy love of a romantic partnership. I've had two long term relationships and they both followed a pattern of being off and on. Breaking up and then getting back together. I now want to find someone to have a healthy adult relationship where they know where I'm coming from. I have a vision of what I would like and what kind of person I'd like to date. The one thing I've always wanted was to be happily married. Although at the age of 53 I haven't given up that dream. But with everything I've been through I don't know how marriage would be for me; I've been alone for a long time.

The Awakening

After leaving high school I went to college for a while but didn't finish. I ended up working as a waitress at a very popular restaurant where I became best friends with Juliette at 23 years old. We would work for 6 months during the summer season and sometimes go places in the winter. Juliette and I have had many fun adventures traveling together. I have met many people along the way. Along with partying at the time and making lifetime memories. She has been my best friends for 30 years and there are more adventures for us in the future.

I was living with roommates including Juliette when I had a breakdown at age 32. I don't remember much of it, but I had been very mean I was told. No one had realized how fragile I really was. I ended up going to the hospital and stayed there for a month. I came out with medicine that I'm still on today. I would really like in the future to go all holistic. I did good for a while but decided to stop taking the medicine and ended up in the hospital again. This time I stayed on the medicine.

I truly believe all of this happened because of the memories I had suppressed about my stepfather. I had a total of 3 breakdowns. To be honest I never wanted to be on these meds. In 2005 I found a healing modality called reiki I fell in love. I got what's called an attunement to channel the healing energy through my hands. I've been told that by doing reiki on others you are healing yourself at the same time. One of my desires in this life is to heal as many people as I can.

That's why I became a massage therapist in 2015. I do have to say doing massages relaxes me just as it does my clients. Not only does massage help me but so does talk therapy. The medicine helps even though I'd rather be all holistic. The talk therapy only goes so far. I believe in clearing of the energy as well. Going through everything I have has made me more compassionate and loving towards others. My best friend said I went through everything with grace. I can see how I've grown as a person, and I love helping others.

Lessons

I've learned many hard lessons along the way. I could not understand why everything happened to me the way it did. It has shaped me to have a deep empathy for others. I can honestly say I have a kind and generous heart. I have a deep connection and love for animals. My pets bring me an unconditional love that sometimes I don't find elsewhere. They make the darkest day turn right around. It's the purest love there is. I have dog sat for a family for a long time and take great pleasure in it. I also donate my time at an animal shelter.

There are things on my journey I am still learning. Learning that regardless of what happened in my childhood it doesn't have to define me. I have learned to love myself in ways I never have before. I'm back to going to the gym which I haven't done in years. I am dealing with my emotions in a healthier way, which in the past I stuffed down with food or alcohol. I'm starting to have more boundaries and learning slowly to stand up for myself which I've always had trouble with.

I've met some really great people along the way. I know some are in my life for a period of time whether it be long term or shorter term. I am grateful for all the lessons and blessings that have happened.

I consider myself a lucky person in a lot of ways. I get to continue on my healing journey that I love and I get to share my story and my experiences with others. We don't always know deep down inside what some people have been through. There are always new lessons to learn. There are always more blessings around the corner. I am not a religious person, but I am a spiritual one. I am open minded and allow my spirituality to grow.

Self Care

I would like to work more on personal self-development. I am always looking for ways to improve myself. I also have weight to release and aim to eat as healthily as I can. Sometimes I eat junk when emotions start to rise up. I know that having the extra weight has kept me safe in my mind. But the weight has given me some health issues I should not have. So now I take full responsibility. Thankfully I gave up alcohol a long time ago but next is eliminating sugar. I also gave up smoking cigarettes twenty years ago. I'm thankful I gave those vices up.

I do forgive myself for the mistakes I have made in my life. The good thing is we learn and grow. The baby steps turn into bigger steps. I would say I have no regrets but that would not be true. I've always wanted to have children; I really would have loved that. I was told by an ex I would make a great Mom. He wanted to have kids right away at twenty four years old but I was nowhere near where I wanted to be financially. We stayed together until we were thirty-eight years old, and he came home and told me he was never going to give me what I wanted most which was kids and marriage, and I was devastated. There were red flags throughout the whole relationship which I ignored. I know I deserve to be happy. They say we are only here for a short time, well I want to make the most of what I have left.

Self Development

I have been to a live personal development workshop with Tony Robbins which was fantastic in itself. There are so many layers to me it feels like I've only just scratched the surface. He did teach me the importance of gratitude. I do fall short sometimes as I am human. He taught me to have grace. The days were long, but we took breaks to dance. We cried it out and screamed it out. We connected with others on a deeper level. It was great experience, and I would do it again. I The next time I would go for my reiki business. I would recommend Tony Robbins teachings for lasting changes. Seeing him was a gift from Juliette as she knows how I like to improve myself when I can.

I wish I would have stated taking care of myself sooner, but I started when I was finally ready. Seeing him in 2022 had helped me to navigate my life a little differently. I've come to realize that many people struggle with childhood trauma or even adult trauma. People have suffered abuse that no one should have to endure. Knowing this, I treat people how I want to be treated. I have a lot to be thankful for-I have work, I have a safe home to go home to, there's always food on my table. I have what others may be dreaming of.

Family

At the age I am now I have put all the foolishness of my youth behind me. I am at an age now where I want to give more and experience more. People have always been meaningful to me, but time is more precious now. I didn't think about when I was younger that people will not be around forever. My Dad who passed at the age of 55 in the year 2000 left me with a broken heart. I knew he had cancer but in my naive mind he was going to be okay until I got the phone call, he was on life support. This changed the axis of my world. It just didn't affect me, but it also affected my little sister Jordan. Jordan is smart, kind and a special needs teacher which is special in itself. She is a good Mom and an all-round good person who has a good sense of humor. These are all the things I've learned about her because we have not met in person yet, but we will. Our story is that we have the same father and different mothers. I'm happy to have her as my sister and I look forward to meeting her and her son Ian soon.

True Love

Life doesn't always make sense to me. In my mind I was going to be married by twenty five and have kids shortly after. I don't really know the why of it. When I see couples that have been together a very long time, I think how lovely they must be- growing old together. I've made some wrong choices in love but when you don't love yourself how can someone else love you? I did not have any relationships to compare what real love looked like from growing up. I know now I deserve so much more. I deserve true love and a healthy partnership. I don't know if I would call myself a hopeless romantic and I do know I have plenty of love from family and friends but I'm yearning for a little more. I want the deep connection of two people really in love. To have that special person to come home to. The special person just for me. This time I know what I want and what I don't want. No more settling for me. I am open to the possibilities!

The Possibilities

One day soon I would like to open my own healing business online and in person. Giving reiki and teaching reiki. This is one of my main goals for 2025. Another goal is to take Juliette on a big adventure to Europe. Also, we are going on a cruise to the Bahamas. I plan on practicing more self-love and more healing myself so I can heal others. The world is wide open for me to experience. I plan on more love from friends and family. With the great possibilities of true love. I plan on being prosperous in all my endeavors. I look forward to my future.

If any of you would like to join me on my healing journey my You Tube channel is called Spirit of Divine Reiki. I also have a business page called Live Good with Leigh on Facebook for anyone wanting a new business alongside me.

Thank you for taking the time out to read my story,

Leigh Stierle

Chapter Twenty-two

By Donna Talbot

Where It All Began

I was born in York in 1979. I have always had a positive outlook on life. I have had a rough ride, and a sad story just like a lot of people. I have always worked hard; I remember helping my Nanna clean at Tang Hall WMC aged 4. I loved helping her and she was my idol. My nanna had 9 children, and I loved her very much. My Nanna was a widow as my grandad had a heart attack aged 54 leaving 9 children behind. He was a wheeler and dealer type of man who used to stay at home to look after the kids. My nanna used to work which was unheard of in those days and iron my grandad shirts every night when she got home. He was a smart man and when she would come home, he would go for a drink in town.

Two of my cousins went into foster care for setting a house on fire and some of my cousins got sold to other family members. I always questioned who I was and had nightmares about if my mum was my mum or my auntie. I never felt loved as a child and maybe that is why I am so cold towards my children; I try so hard not to be, I love my children very much.

One day a man came knocking on the door hounding my mum for a date. He put his foot in the door, and she was trying to shut him out. I whispered in her ear, "just pretend you'll go and don't turn up," he said, "what did she say?" and my mum told him. I felt betrayed. I was only 4 years old.

The Journey

That night I woke up from a nightmare and I went out onto the landing crying my eyes out looking for my mum. This fat ugly naked man appeared and said, "she's downstairs." Then I heard my mum in a stern voice say from her room "I'm here." I went to snuggle in next to her, but she dragged me back into my room and said, "if you don't shut your mouth I'll leave you." This haunted me 40 years later going through menopause.

We moved house in the middle of the night. It was dark and my mum had gotten with the neighbour's son who was 18 at the time. His mother used to torture us kids while they were at the pub, throwing stones at the window shouting abuse. My mum came back from the pub one night and ended up fighting with her in the front garden. My stepdad aka pops was a rebel stealing cars and motorbikes. The police came once and searched the house. They were just about to leave, and I said, "They've not looked in my play cupboard under the floorboards." I thought I was helping but no off to jail he went.

Then we moved to Tedder Road. I was so happy at Tedder Road. I enjoyed my childhood, but my mum started smoking weed and my stepdad was on speed. We got raided by the police and my stepdad was in and out of jail. We always had the best of everything due to the criminal activity, and I had a TV and stereo in my room. My mum used to always want me to sleep in her bed with her when my stepdad was in jail. When he got out, I had to go back in my own bed, and I felt rejected and used. I try not to let any of my own boys' sleep with me in case I meet someone as I do not want them to feel the same.

My mum let me stay out at my friend's house down Thorsby Road once. Her mum and her stepdad came back drunk arguing, and he started battering her and smashing the house up. We were both frightened to death and trying to figure a way out. She was trying to stick up for her mum and me, but he started shouting abuse at us. Everything went quiet and my friend told me to run and get help. It was the middle of the night and there no mobile phones then. I was in my PJ's, and I never ran so fast in all my life. Luckily, I lived around the corner, and they were still up- thank god. They all ran round to help, and they couldn't believe the state of the house; smashed to bits top to bottom, it looked more like a burglary.

In Year 6 I got bullied by my class. I used to go home sick most days and my mother was up at school complaining. Nothing happened until my mum, again my hero, went and knocked on all the parents' doors and said, "if it doesn't stop, I'm going to bray you." I loved my mum for sticking up for me!

My real dad Derek used to turn up drunk asking to take me out. I never understood why they stopped me from seeing him. If they'd told me the truth I would have understood. He used to bring me 2p's and I thought he was the dogs' bollocks. He arranged to take me to Flamingo Land one day and I sat on the doorstep waiting for him to come. My mum said he wasn't coming but I waited until late looking out of the window and feeling abandoned and let down. I remember looking for him one day and I found him in a bedsit in town. I cried on his shoulder asking what I'd done wrong and why did he not want to see me. The feeling of not being important left me feeling rejected, abandoned, unloved, and unwanted.

Growing Up

My first job was at Hudson's hotel Bootham aged 15 as a Chambermaid. Then I did my work experience at Swallow Hotel Tadcaster Road. I made lifelong friends there. I was a chef de rang at 19, but my true passion was travel. I got a job with one of the number 1 airlines at the time as a Transfer Rep. By this time, I had met my son Tyler's dad who liked a drink. I'd been offered my dream job, and I went for it. I found out I was pregnant, and I still went for my dream job. I was carrying

The Journey

my 2 suitcases up flights of stairs after 3 months of working out there when I lost the baby. It wasn't meant to be, and I came home because I missed my family. Dave and my uncle were there to greet me. I was in love with Dave who was sofa surfing at the time in and out of work and taking drugs on a weekend. I went to Casalocos as I loved the music and how ecstasy made me feel, and I went on to get pregnant with Tyler.

I was working at JD Sports where my friend and I experienced sexual harassment. At the time Dave had done what Dave does best, a disappearing act for 3 months, and I did not have a clue what was going on with us. Were we together or not? My mum and my nanna ended up helping me buy stuff for the baby. I was pregnant and Dave did not find pregnant woman attractive.

We used to go shopping to Netto every Friday night and then Dave would disappear for the weekend, and I'd be housebound with the baby. This went on for 2 years. It was my 21st birthday and I had a limo booked for me and my friends. The limo arrived and Dave was late. When I said "you're late, my friends are waiting" he spat in my face a few times. So, I wiped my face and went out with my friends, and we had the best laugh ever. I'd had enough of Daves disappearing acts and I really thought he was cheating. I went to the flat and tried kicking the door down. He came to the door telling me I was crazy. The next time I went out I slept with someone else and was happy to tell him what I did thinking he'd blurt out his cheating over the years. But instead, I got no reaction so it must have been a relief that it was the end of us.

Tyler started smashing his room up at 2 years old, and he got a diagnosis at age 5/6 of ADHD. He was hard work, and I just wanted to go out and have fun with my friends. I was lost and lonely. My choice in men after Dave went downhill, and I was getting hammered waking up with Tom, Dick, or Harry desperate to be loved by all the wrong people.

Domestic Abuse Starts

I was working cash in hand jobs and met a travelling man. He said he was divorced and showed me divorce papers to prove it. He was a lot older than me; I was around 26 and he was in his 40's. He was there for me and took me to Whitby for the weekend and took me shopping and bought me clothes. Then he said he was going back to his wife. It was Tyler's birthday the next day and who came knocking on the door wanting to spend Tyler's birthday- Dave. We ended up in bed together and the travelling man broke in through the downstairs window. I told Dave to get in bed with Tyler and act normal. The traveller had been on drink and coke and ran into Tyler's room throwing punches. I was worried he would miss Dave and hit my son, so I jumped on the travellers back. Dave ran out of the bedroom, jumped over the banister and down into the street in his boxers. The traveller threw a punch at me. My nose started bleeding, and an ambulance and police arrived. I lost all respect for Dave for just running away.

After that, I got with one of my so-called friends Glen. He was 6ft tall and made me feel protected and safe. I was a lap dancer at the time, and he used to give me lifts to Wildcats in Wakefield. As soon as we were a couple everything changed. He became a control freak, and it was 5 years of hell. I lost 2 babies with him. With the first nothing grew in the sack, but the 2nd time I was 14 weeks pregnant and was told that the baby had died inside me at 12 weeks. It was awful and they told me to go home and let it pass. I said no to the scan picture and requested a D and C. I ended up with bell's palsy at age of 26 due to the tortured stress he put me through. I've never been the same since and lost all my confidence. He let me go out with my friends and then would torture me, following me around the house asking who I'd cheated on him with. This went on all day and night until I gave him the answer he wanted as I could not cope with the stress.

He strangled me a few times and I'd pass out. Tyler witnessed him trying to cut my hand with a knife and strangling me whilst pouring lemonade in my face. My heart bleeds for Tyler who stood at the top of the stairs and wet himself in fear. I had to get away from this monster but every time I tried to break away I couldn't. He would throw pints over me and my sister in town, point and pull his finger across his throat, make death threats to me, my family and my neighbour's daughter who babysat. He pulled a knife on her and told her not to babysit again. He also slashed every tyre on my car number of times.

One Christmas he took all of the presents family had bought for Tyler back. How can you do that to an infant? I was pregnant with Harley at the time, and it was easier to stay, but I was not losing another baby to that monster. He started hitting me in the belly and I broke free. I got panic alarms in the house and went to domestic abuse courses.

He'd done something bad to one of his cousins. I went to the toilet and pulled his jacket off the toilet door so I could have a piss in peace and a gun went off in his pocket. It could have fired in any direction. I went into fight of flight mode, took my high heel off and hit him over head with it. Blood started trickling down his face and I ran as fast as I could out the house.

Now 7 months pregnant I was on my own and protecting my unborn child. I had pelvic separation and was on crutches. My sister was with me and my mum was by my side like always. I had my 2nd c-section, and they cut into my bladder by accident. I thought I was going to die on that operating table, I lost so much blood. Glen wanted to come and see the baby, but I refused until he was around 4 months old and mainly did it for his nana and auntie.

He asked me to take him to Farm Foods shopping and whilst there asked me if I'd slept with someone else. I said, "yes on my uncles sofa," and he picked Harley up out of the trolly, dragged me out by my hair and started smashing my head against the car. He got me in the back of the car, and he kept turning his head and hitting and slapping me. I thought we were going to crash. My mum rang and he said, "you'll get your daughter back when I have finished with her." My stepdads brother Leon was at my mum's house, and he came round to confront Glen. I got out shaking and drove home.

Skip Forward 5 years

Romes's dad and I did not want any more children, but this child saved me in so many ways he is my angel my bestest blessing, thank you universe! Me and Dawon had been friends with benefits in between relationships and we ended up at the same party. We ended up in bed and I accidently got pregnant. I was debating whether to keep the baby or not. He said it would sort him out and get him off drugs. He was funny and I'm funnier.

Dawon was always going on benders, partying at his flat, sleeping behind my back and he sent me crazy! At 7 months pregnant around 2nd or 3rd January 2016 I picked him up from his flat, I'd been working, and he'd been on it when I arrived. We argued and he smashed a glass in my face. My mouth and face were pouring with blood. He rang the police and told them it was domestic abuse. I had to go to hospital on my own. His family were then kissing my arse as they knew he would get deported. I dropped the charges as I wanted him to meet his first child, and I was desperate for him to change. I did not want to do this alone. As it turned out Dawon got his name on birth certificate and fucked off. So here I was with three kids by three different men. All I ever wanted was to be loved but how could someone love me if I did not love myself?

Forgiveness Sets Us Free

After nine years I have forgiven Dawon and we now co-parent. Forgiveness sets us free. I have done Belief Coding with Georgina Kate Wesley and Jess Cunningham. With Gemma Elizabeth Williams I have done ancestral healing, and mother Mary healing, healing past traumas and I am still on my journey of learning to love me first. My dreams are to open a hostel for 16 to 21-year-olds to provide affordable living for young working adults, heal them from past trauma and help them with cooking skills, paperwork and setting healthy boundaries.

I feel like I let my two eldest children down. Tyler was not allowed to live at home and at 15 he ended up on the streets on crack. My nephew had him selling for him, and he ran up a debt in his name so could not live in York. He is now MC Sharkie on YouTube and has turned his life around. I am so proud. Harley listens to his dad now and has changed his last name. He is doing very well with a nice girlfriend and apprenticeship. I wish my sons well and all the success in the world. I love you both very much.

I do not want to hurt anyone in this book. It is a part of me healing and letting go. We all have a choice and I want peace and happiness.

Chapter Twenty-three

By Shirley Bailey

Flying With Grace

I have been a helper since I left school. I have always liked listening and trying to make life better for everyone including myself. My chapter is dedicated to one of my friends who was taken away from the world by the rath of a knife. Unfortunately, she was killed by a stranger- an 18-year-old man. I will explain the details further on below.

I dedicate this chapter to the lady who lost her life. Many will know of my friend Bibaa Henry and because Bibaa Henry and her sister Nicole Smallman were murdered in Brent, London. I also dedicate this chapter to Bibaa's parents, her friends and everyone who knew her and still love her very much. Also, to anyone who has lost someone to knife crime. The sadness changes in time but never leaves you.

The reason for writing this chapter is to help others. The aim of my work has always been to help and try to make a difference to other people. One thing I have learnt when helping people is that the people who come to help you in challenging times are the people who you should have around you all the time. Before I continue, I would like to say thank you Bibaa for being in my life. You are still here and help me to strive to be better.

The Meeting

We met at work. I saw Bibaa sitting in the office waiting for her identification to be confirmed as she had the same job as me. Bibaa sat on her own and it was not clear as to how long she would have to wait. I sat and chatted to Bibaa and made her feel welcome. That was a start of a beautiful friendship. I remember this moment like it was just yesterday. Bibaa had this way about her, she was a lady with a big heart intriguing from the beginning. A little lady who was witty, clever and beautiful all at the same time. She had an infectious laugh and was always happy to get involved in whatever was happening. Once our friendship blossomed, I began to trust and confided in Bibaa when I needed to. She was a little diamond, one of those friends of whom I would never want to lose.

The Friendship

When we worked together it was a great experience. We were like two peas in a pod. Trying to take the same lunch break so that we could chat to each other and catch up on the weekend's shenanigans. She really opened her heart to me as I did with to her. At that time, I worked away from home, and we would meet after work for a drink outside the pub right by our workplace. We would laugh and joke for an hour or two spending the time trying to put the world to rights. One time after work we sat with a drink and some Morris dancers came to the pub of course me and Bibaa had to have a go. Thats the kind of friendship that anyone would want.

Bibaa would sit and listen to my experiences of trying to find somewhere to stay during the week and ending up in some situations where I was really living out of a suitcase. I could only talk things through with Bibaa as she was the only one who really understood.

The Heartache

Early on a Monday morning whilst I was working alone during a lockdown the phone rang. The person who had called asked if I knew Bibaa. They went on to tell me that Bibaa had been murdered. Nothing could prepare me for what was to come. She could not say any more as there was a police investigation. However, she said that I should watch the news which may give me more information.

I turned on my television and waited for the news only to hear that two women had been murdered in a park in Brent. I knew it was Bibaa's birthday, and she had planned to go to a park with her friends. I did not go due to Covid 19 and being in lockdown. I could not believe my eyes and felt heartbroken. I did not know how this had happened and most of all why someone would do this. I felt a deep sadness. I was all alone. My heart was aching, broken, I had no answers and did not understand. I just sat confused, upset, and bewildered. Not knowing what to do next.

I tried to carry on working but found it really hard to concentrate. Not sure what to do or how this had happened. I spent the day watching the news to see if I could find out anything more to help me understand what had happened. But unfortunately, there was nothing. The only thing that I could do was take to the internet. I kept searching. At first it was almost daily and then monthly. The photo that was on the news which for me stuck out the most was that of Bibaa and Nicole dancing with fairy lights around them. That saddened me as I knew that if I was there, I would have also been dancing with them and on the picture. But would that murderer have stood a chance if there was three of us? I will never know the answer to that. I know for many other people there are a lot of unanswered questions too.

It was Bibaa's sister's boyfriend who had found the bodies hidden in bushes and full of stab wounds. I knew like me Bibaa would not have gone down without a fight. She was small in stature but like me she could stand up for herself. But it was dark maybe she would never have stood a chance. I then started to think that if I was there, we could have fought that person together. I was in disbelief that my friend had been taken away from me. No more weekly telephone conversations about what we would be doing in our future and no more plans to go on holiday together. Our time together was over.

I then started to see comments online about my friend and started to see that strangers were making comments about the sisters and how they had different skin colours. These comments sent me into a rage, and I then started my own campaign online to stop the comments of which I did not like and tried to correct people. They knew nothing about the sisters so who were they to make comments about strangers? My heart was broken again and again. I did not know how much more I could take. The sadness was awful, and the mixed emotions of anger really did get to me. Why? Thats all I kept asking myself. But I was not responsible for those horrible comments, and I knew that any words that I wrote would stop those comments.

The pain then just got worse. About a year later I saw again on the news that police officers had sent some pictures of the crime scene and my friend's body in a WhatsApp group. This sent me backwards. This was for me misogyny at its worst. I could only imagine how from what I had heard that the photo's must have contained images of one of my friends' bodies in what I could only describe to be in an horrific condition. This was not how anyone would want their friend to be seen.

Their behaviour is despicable and when my friend was at her worst not down to her own doing, they then humiliated her even further. I can only say that those police officers devalued my friend and her sister. As I write this there are tears in my eyes. My refection's of this are that the police did not even consider the consequences of their behaviour on others and in this case, ignorance should not have been an option. Again, I was lost all alone and full of grief. I then recalled how Bibaa's family would have felt and imagined that Bibaa would be shocked by what had happened. Knowing Bibaa and remembering what she was like gave me the courage to go on.

I struggle to write this. I know that I must continue as if one person reads this and chooses to put a knife down from reading this then I have done what I intended to do. My aim is not to offend anyone who knew Bibaa, and do not take away the fact that they loved and knew Bibaa more than me. It is difficult to comprehend why someone would kill my friend.

Learning To Overcome Things

I have no idea why people decide to carry a knife but what is clear it that if you carry one you will use it. A plan or unplanned incident is very likely to happen. But no one thinks of the sadness that is left behind. Knowing Bibaa she would not want anyone to suffer. She would want me to be strong carry on with my life and be grateful for life. Through all the difficulties I had to accept what had happened. I felt a very big loss and pain because of the experience she has been through. I really struggled to comprehend why someone could do this to my beautiful friend.

What Happens Next

I then started to share memories of Bibaa with anyone who would listen. This was a struggle but helped me as most people knew who I was talking about as Bibaa and Nicole were on the national news. To keep Bibaa's memory alive I began to buy little things with Bee's on. Bibaa loved bees.

As soon as I saw in the news that the person had killed my friend and her sister, I visited the park in Brent, London. I wrote a sympathy card and put it in a picture frame. The card was blue in colour, and I wrote on it 'gone too soon'. I drove there alone and went to one of the gates in the park. I lit a candle and said a prayer remembering my friend.

The Journey

But at the same time, I was overcome by sadness. I reflected on the friendship that I had with Bibaa and how much I missed her. I was honest with people close to me about how angry I felt. I recalled the positive memories that I had of her and began to take care of myself. I did this by completing meditation each evening and lighting candles that smelled nice. After the person who did this was caught, I felt a sense of release and continued to search for further information.

Bibaa was a fighter. She would stand up for everyone's rights and so I did the same for Bibaa. I made a complaint against the police. This complaint was responded to on the same night. I could not get my head around why police officers had taken pictures of my friend. So, then I progressed to making a complaint to the local MP, but this went nowhere. I felt let down by not only the police but also by an MP. At this stage I questioned everything and began to question who I could trust. Overcome by grief I guess I was trying to find answers.

The question that I kept asking myself was why and what I could do to help things. When the reality at that time was that I was stuck alone inside my home due to covid 19 and that really, I could not do anything because I had not killed Bibaa.

I carried on in my helping role and began to feel differently about the world and my view of it. I worked from home and informed my manager at that time what had happened. To help me not react to things I came out of a work WhatsApp group. This meant that I would not respond to anyone inappropriately. I had difficulties in eating and sleeping at first. I felt so broken that even trivial things that needed completing became difficult.

I went to the funeral but could not go in the church as it was full. So, there was a lot of people outside of the church. I travelled to the funeral alone and cried outside of the church. I went home alone. Then always when the sun came out after this I would spend as much time as I could sitting in my garden listening to music. There is a glass that I have from the same pub that we used to buy a drink from, and I would drink from that. There were many tears that were held alone and unseen.

Each year on her birthday and the day when she was murdered, I remember Bibaa. Once the person who murdered Bibaa and Nicole was captured things began to settle for me. I recall that I worried about Bibaa parents, our friends and her family. I remembered how kind Bibaa was and our shopping trips at lunch time. Bibaa's words of wisdom always helped me to get through things. There were times during covid that I would not see anyone. I found myself working late into the night so I would not have to deal with my thoughts. When we had long phone calls for over two hours it was a joy.

I then started to journal and write a poem about how I felt and how much I missed Bibaa. I lit a candle for Bibaa on a regular basis. When I feel like I am losing my way with things I make my way back to my fridge where a picture and a poem about Bibaa is placed and remember that laugh and smile from Bibaa.

As years went by, and the case came to trial the newspapers, and the TV further reported on the matter. Bibaa then came back to the forefront of my mind again. I thought I had learnt to cope with my loss. But seeing pictures of Bibaa almost daily when the trial was being heard was a lot to cope with. I wanted my friend back who sat outside with me drinking a glass of cider after work. Everything became harder until a verdict was heard. I was very angry.

I do not know how I got through this. But I did. The loss of a friend is not really taken seriously. You are not offered leave from work and people think "Oh it's just a friend. She'll be ok." A true friendship is something that I hold onto. I can only say that I have never experienced sadness like this before.

How I Coped

I treasure the friendship I had with Bibaa. Bibaa's picture remains on my fridge and every morning and night her memory is with me. I see her beautiful face which makes me smile and remember the nice times that we had together.

I now recognise that I have the right to feel angry when I want. Sometimes when I walk or sit outside, I look up to the stars wondering where we would both be now if she was still here. No one prepares us for the journey we go through when we lose someone that we love.

I have not really had many experiences of dealing with those emotions of losing someone. I went into a state of depression. My friends said that I could always talk to them, but I did not want to place that burden on them. There were days when I would dream about Bibaa and then wake up with a cold sweat, nausea and feeling anxious. To help me through this I would then complete some morning meditations. This helped me a lot.

I then began to read books on grief and loss and how to cope with this. I soon began to feel less alone, and I treasure the times that I had with Bibaa. I also googled low-cost counselling sessions but have never felt ready to take this up as I did not want to bring everything back up again.

Every time I hear, see, or read something about knife crime it subconsciously takes me back to when my friend and her sister was murdered. It overwhelms me with painful sorrow and anger. The pain is mental and physical as my head hurts and has been hurting whilst writing this. I have learnt to acknowledge my emotions of anger and learnt not to let this was fester inside me.

So, I now try to help others who have a belief that it is right to carry a knife for self-protection. There is no protection that a knife can offer anyone because one slip and it can kill. But in this case, it was a plan to kill 6 women, and the reality is that Bibaa and her sister were in the wrong place at the wrong time.

All I ask is do not buy that knife or use one.

Printed in Great Britain
by Amazon